Don't
FILL UP
On the Antipasto

Tony Danza's Father-Son Cookbook

*With Memories of an Italian-American Family
and 50 of Their Best Recipes*

Tony and Marc Danza

SCRIBNER

New York London Toronto Sydney

SCRIBNER
A Division of Simon & Schuster, Inc.
1230 Avenue of the Americas
New York, NY 10020

First Scribner hardcover edition May 2008

SCRIBNER and design are trademarks of The Gale Group, Inc., used under license
by Simon & Schuster, the publisher of this work.

For information about special discounts for bulk purchases,
please contact Simon & Schuster Special Sales at 1-800-456-6798
or business@simonandschuster.com

Manufactured in the United States of America

1   3   5   7   9   10   8   6   4   2

Library of Congress Control Number: 2007046878

ISBN-13: 978-1-4165-4487-6
ISBN-10: 1-4165-4487-9

We dedicate this book,
with love,
to Matty Iadanza and the Camisas.
A great man and one hell of a family.

CONTENTS

Pasta

Main Courses

FOREWORD

Tony Danza is not only a talented actor but also an incredible friend who shines in the kitchen and is not shy about sharing his talents with friends. Take it from me—if you haven't tasted Tony's meatballs, you haven't lived! His meatballs are exquisite! His lasagna ain't bad either!

I recall with great pleasure the first time I experienced Tony's cooking. Tony and I, with our respective others, were at a glamorous Hollywood party where they were serving an elaborate buffet of Italian food. I helped myself to a plate of lasagna and told Tony, "This is great. You've got to have some."

Tony tried the lasagna, gave me a pitying look, and said, "You think this is lasagna? You've gotta be kidding!"

We both laughed about it, but the next day who should arrive at my house carrying a large dish of lasagna and a container filled with homemade meatballs? Yes, Tony Danza! I have to say it was a great culinary experience.

Tony is an amazing cook because he puts his heart and soul into it. Growing up in Brooklyn, he learned to cook from his father, Matty. Tony would wander around the kitchen while his father prepared all kinds of delicious Italian feasts. He would watch and he would learn. His beloved mother, Anna, encouraged him, and Tony took it from there. So . . . all I can say is if you want great meatballs, sensational lasagna, or anything else Italian—Tony Danza is your man! *Oh yes, and he gives great barbecue too!* I unfortunately have not had the pleasure of tasting his son Marc's cooking, but considering his lineage, I hope I do.

Jackie Collins

Don't **FILL UP** On the Antipasto

IN THE BEGINNING

Originally the title of this book was *Father and Son Cooking, Keeping Family Traditions Alive, or, Gee, I Hate to Waste a Good Salad.* We knew that title was way too long, and our editor said it would never fit on any cover. But my son and I wanted a title that summed up what we were going for with the book. We wanted our cookbook to be more than just recipes. Of course, it would have to have great recipes, some easy, some not so easy, but we also wanted the book to tell a little bit about why we cook, why we love to cook, and where our love for cooking comes from. The answer to all three questions is our wonderful family and the traditions that they honored and that we continue to honor. Most of those traditions, if not all of them, revolved around food. So this book we hope will be, above all, a good cookbook that is also entertaining and serves as a window into our wonderful family and the characters in it. And we do mean characters.

We didn't get our first title, but we would still like to use its three parts as sort of an outline and to explain what those parts mean to us. The first part is *Father and Son Cooking*. That is exactly what my son and I did in writing this book. *We cooked together. We ate together. We also remembered together and, oh, did we laugh together.* Marc reminded me of things I hadn't thought of in years or had completely forgotten, and I did the same for him. One other thing about cooking with your son—it's a really great way to bond and I do love him so. We may argue over an ingredient or two, but when we sit down to eat what we've made together, there is nothing like it.

Now, unlike in most Italian families, my father did almost all the cooking. It was there, watching my father in the kitchen, that I learned to love to cook, and my son later learned the same way, by watching me. An interesting thing happens when you see your father in the kitchen, cooking. It's no longer just woman's work, and there is no stigma attached to cooking or being in the kitchen. Even though I loved watching him, I never realized how hard it was to make dinner for a family of four every night. He had to come up with the menu, get the ingredients, prepare the food, and make sure my brother, my mother, and I had something good to eat, every night.

I discovered Marc's love of cooking early on and he got right into it. I remember his first attempt at frying eggs. He wanted them over easy. The problem was we almost lost our little house in the Hollywood Hills. There was nothing easy about those eggs. The fireman did like the coffee he made, though. Marc now has a son of his own, and as you can see from the front cover, he's already cooking. My grandson's a fast learner. As I said, I learned from my father and what I learned were his Old World recipes. My son is a bit more adventuresome in the kitchen, but more about that later.

I learned the way my father made *the* meatballs, the way he made soup, the way he made sausage and peppers, and, of course, the way made *the* sauce. *You will notice throughout this book that some of the food has a* the *in front of it. For example,* the *lasagna. Not just lasagna, but* the *lasagna. This designation is for the very special dishes, the ones that have a special place in our family and many Italian families.* So what I learned from my father was a love for cooking, but just as importantly, he took the fear out of it. One of the things you learn when you spend some time in the kitchen is that cooking is a lot of fun, and it's pretty hard to mess up. It's also Zen-like, in that when you're chopping garlic, that's pretty much all you can think about. My father taught me some basic rules and I passed them on to my son. He said cook with good, fresh ingredients and stay away from processed food as much as possible. Have a little patience when you cook and you'll have a good experience and you'll get to eat too.

While we are on the subject of ingredients, it's important to us that we convey a message of mindful eating. As you know in our country today, and all over the world, obesity has become an epidemic. In today's paper, as we write this, there is an article that says even modestly overweight baby boomers will live shorter lives. So it's time to start thinking about what we eat. There was this legend in our family that as long as they ate peasant food, meaning fresh fruits, vegetables, pastas, and really not much meat, they stayed healthy. As they moved into the middle class, their diets changed. They blamed their later illnesses not on age but on what they ate. Whether they were right or wrong, you are what you eat—so consider that next time you start to chew. Sounds good to us.

The second part of our original title is *Keeping Family Traditions Alive*. This is important. I talked earlier about my father, Matty, making dinner every night for my family. We now know how important it is that families have dinner together. Numerous studies have shown that when kids eat dinner with their parents, they are much less likely to get into trouble. The more nights a week you eat together, the better. This is a family tradition that both my son and I try to honor. It's a great time to interact with your kids and find out what's going on in their lives. My parents made us talk at the dinner table, I made my kids talk, and as soon as Marc's son, Nicholas, can talk, he'll be talking too. *News flash: My grandson just called me Grandpa, well, actually, "Grampna." We are so excited.*

The big tradition that we try to keep alive is Sunday dinner. Sunday dinner was always important at our house, but it was made more important because my mother's father and mother, my maternal grandparents, lived in the apartment downstairs. First of all, it is an incredible thing to have your grandparents around as you're growing up. I wish my daughters could have had more of that. My dad, unfortunately, was gone before the girls were born. My mom passed when Katie was five and Emily was an infant. Luckily my wife's parents are still around and are a big part of the girls' lives. Marc was lucky to spend a lot of time with my mother when he was growing up. He lived with her on Long Island while he went to school there. She told me it was good for him and a thrill for her. Having your grandparents around also means that the aunts and the uncles with their kids, "the cousins," come and visit and most of all on Sunday for dinner. When I woke up on Sunday morning, I could smell the meatballs frying in garlic and oil. They were always so great to eat for breakfast before my father put them in the sauce. Three generations later my grandson, Nicholas, wakes up to that smell on Sunday mornings. My son, Marc, though, doesn't only cook like me and I'm glad about that. He makes a great meatball, and that is the true test, but as you'll see later in the book he is also a creative cook. One of the joys of cooking is making your own dishes and making dishes your own, and let me tell you, Marc makes a terrific mango salsa. Since this part of the old title is about family, we'd like to introduce you to some of the Camisa family. The Camisas. My mother's side of the family.

My grandparents were Anna and Tony and my mother and father were Anna and Matty. My mother had five brothers and sisters: our uncles John, Tony, and Mike, and our aunts Rose and Fran. Their spouses were Anne, Josie, Sadie, Vinny, and Phil. Just writing all the names made us laugh. They were so great and so important to us. Especially to me as I grew up. One of the best things about having Marc at such a young age is that he got to grow up around these wonderful people too. It is a great gift to grow up around loving and fun uncles and aunts.

On a roof in Brooklyn, after the war. *Back row, left to right:* Aunt Sadie, my father's mother, his brother Louie, my mother's mother, Anna, and father, Tony *Front row, left to right:* Uncle Mike, my mom, and Uncle Tony

In all I had nineteen first cousins, and we grew up much like siblings because the family was always together. How I looked forward to the family gatherings! Fortunately they happened all the time. My mother's side would take turns having dinners and get-togethers. They were sometimes at Uncle Vinny and Aunt Rose's place in Patchogue, which was like the country for us city kids, sometimes at Aunt Frances and Uncle Phil's in Lynbrook, or at Uncle Mike and Aunt Sadie's, or at our house (first on Euclid Avenue in Brooklyn and later in Malverne, Long Island). These were great times. The whole family together. My aunts, uncles, and cousins. All so close. I especially got a kick out of my older cousins, who were so cool and whom I idolized. Throughout this book we will try to remember some of these people with stories that connect the recipes with our sweet memories.

•   •   •

The last part of the title is *Gee, I Hate to Waste a Good Salad*, which I heard from my dad almost every night after dinner. As Marc grew up he heard it from me, and I am sure his son will hear it from him. Where does this saying come from? Almost every night, as we cleared the dinner table, my father would stand at the kitchen sink eating the last bits of salad out of the salad bowl—that last bit of crispy lettuce, a slice of onion, a wedge of cucumber. Then he would say, as he shook his head, "Gee, I hate to waste a good salad." It's a silly little memory, but it stays with us for some reason. *These are the kind of memories that this book is about. Remembering good times and good food with the people you love.* This book is about cooking with your son or any of your other relatives or friends. It's about

The aunts and uncles
Back row, left to right: my mom, Uncle John, Aunt Rose, Uncle Tony, Aunt Sadie, Uncle Mike, and Uncle Phil
Front row, left to right: Aunt Anne, Aunt Fran, and Aunt Josie

eating with your family and about the connection of food and family and the joys of a happy family life. It's about making sure the traditions that bind you together stay alive and strong. We hope you enjoy the book, the pictures, and most of all, the recipes. And we hope you find the same joy in reading and using this book that we found in writing it.

Look! We did have fun.

WORDS FROM THE SON

When my father asked me to write a cookbook with him, I was excited and a little apprehensive. I wondered, Could we do this? Do we have enough recipes? What else would we talk about in the book? He told me his idea, that we would make it a homage to our family. I started to think about all the great people and food I had grown up with. I thought about my aunt Rose cooking sauce in a small hot kitchen on Long Island every Sunday. I thought about my grandfather Matty making veal cutlets and my grandmother Anna cooking me a steak and trying to get me to eat her beets. I thought about my father saying every time, when he finished whatever Italian food he made, "Send a picture to Italy and tell them this is what it's supposed to look like!"

I have so many memories of my father in the kitchen. I remember him cooking me egg sandwiches in the morning and singing Sinatra songs while flipping the egg in the air. Another favorite memory is the pizza dough he would prepare the night before. In the morning the dough would be spilling over the bowl onto the counter, and he would be humming away getting ready to make some of the best pizza

I have ever eaten. I also thought about my mother-in-law, Joyce Frattalone, cooking her sauce, with Pasquale, her husband, making the meatballs right next to her. I should tell you that I was so lucky to have married a wonderful Italian girl named Julie. Her family has so many of the same traditions we do. Sunday pasta, of course, is my favorite. I thought, What luck. I get excellent Sunday pasta in Minnesota too. Like our family, they also serve pasta alongside the turkey on Thanksgiving. It was so nice to feel at home when I was so far from home, and I know Julie feels the same way too. *I could go on and on with memories of relatives and friends enjoying themselves in the kitchen, cooking like they didn't have a care in the world.* So why not write a cookbook that includes wonderful stories, memories, and, of course, recipes from our lives?

Once my father and I actually started writing the book, memories were jarred that made us laugh, chuckle, and even cry. We looked through old photos of our beloved relatives and were reminded how many are no longer with us. Both of my Iadanza grandparents, Uncle John, Uncle Tony, Uncle Vinny, Uncle Mike, Aunt Rose, and Cousin Patty have passed. We realized how important it was to write this cookbook. We needed to flesh out those old characters from our past that had such an impact on our lives. We could then give our children a piece of our family history that they, unfortunately, were not around to experience.

Another thought about writing this book with my father was, Hey, could we actually sit down with each other and work

Our Christmas card in Hollywood Hills, 1980. I bought some snow.

every day? We had done segments on his talk show together, and I did act in a couple episodes of *Taxi* when I was younger, but writing a cookbook with him seemed a daunting task. We have a great relationship (don't get me wrong) but a working relationship is another story. When it comes to work, he has his particulars and I have mine. I am a computer guy, he is a pen guy. I like to work in the morning, and he likes to work out in the morning and then work in the afternoon. So, on the first day we planned to work, we met around 11 A.M. at his house. We sat down at the table and stared blankly at each other.

My father asked, "How should we do this?"

I said, "I don't know."

But then out of nowhere we started to just talk about food, relatives, and the past. The next thing we knew it was about an hour and a half later, and we were both amazed at the stories we remembered.

Then we got hungry.

We ate and drank a beer and talked about some of our recipes. By the time evening came we looked at each other and said, "We can do it!" Funny, just then my father got a call from his agent saying he was offered the lead in the Broadway musical *The Producers*. A song from the musical immediately came to mind—"We Can Do It." Subsequently my father took the part and moved to New York. There went the afternoons planned for writing the cookbook. He looked at me and said, "Get this thing organized. My money's on you." So I was given the task of organizing a working copy that we could send back and forth and build into a real draft.

Sitting at the computer, still licking my wounds from a business venture that didn't go as expected, I didn't know where to start. I was working on getting my career back on track, and my father was living his dream of playing the lead in one of the most successful plays in Broadway history. To say we were at opposite ends of the success spectrum would be an understatement. I was lost and struggling to get the gist of the book. I know what you're thinking, It's a cookbook! But I wanted, as my father did, for this book to be more than just recipes. We wanted to feel proud of our family history. We wanted the great food we grew up with to continue. I went to New York to see the play and stayed with my father while we worked on the book during the month of February. Needless to say, seeing your father on Broadway is a huge thrill. He was amazing, and if you didn't see *The Producers* with him in it, you certainly should kick yourself now. Incredibly, even though he was working and I saw the show every day and twice on Wednesday, we got a lot of work done. As the family stories and recipes started coming, we were on our way. I even learned some new cooking tricks and insider info about Broadway, and my father learned not to trust me to organize.

THE FATHER SPEAKS

I didn't really want to do a cookbook. In fact, the first proposal to do one came while I still had my talk show. It was to be a straight cookbook with me as the sole author. To be honest, I didn't think I warranted a cookbook. I like to cook and I think I'm pretty good at it, but my repertoire is limited. Although, I do love using cookbooks.

Then I had a thought: How about a cookbook from me and my son, Marc? For those who don't know, I was nineteen years old when Marc was born. Literally, we grew up together. He's a great kid and I love him so. (By the way, he now has a great son, Nicholas. He's the kid in the middle, on the cover. Cute, huh?) *So I thought we'd write a father-son cookbook with a big dose of our family added, basically about my father and my mother's whole side of the family. I love that they call it "her side," like it's a sporting event.* I really like that our cookbook pays tribute to our great family, and I think we have some terrific recipes in this book. Some we grew up with, some have evolved since Marc and I started cooking them, and some are new and due primarily to my son's creativity in the kitchen.

To say I have enjoyed writing this book is an understatement. As I said, Marc and I actually grew up together, and we have a very special relationship. Writing this book has made it even better. I didn't think that was possible. First of all, we spent a lot of time together, thinking, remembering, and laughing about times gone by, times we were lucky to have. It was so great when we would remember something we hadn't thought of in so long and to have our memories jogged by each other. We found some great pictures, which we have shared and use to paint a picture of our youth, or as we say in Brooklyn, our "yout."

The other great thing about writing this book was the actual cooking, which we did in our kitchen in California. It's a great kitchen to cook in. And we had help—my dear Hilda and Beatrice, better known as BT (because that's what my daughter Emily called her when she was a baby). Hilda has been with our family for almost thirty years and Beatrice over fifteen, so they really know their way around our kitchen. To tell the truth, we are a cooking drill team. We're not only good but also fast. We can make a Sunday sauce, meatballs, ribs, and a braciole or two in no time flat. If it didn't have to simmer, it would be called fast food.

We cooked everything in the book to make sure it all worked. Cooking and telling people how to cook are two different things. *You're probably wondering what we did with all that food. The answer to that question, of course, is my brother, Matty. We cooked. He ate.* Marc called me on Monday morning, after two full days of cooking, and was marveling at my brother's intake. He was dying to get him on a scale. I told Marc it was

My brother, Matty, watching Marc's every move

a good sign that he ate so much because he only eats what he likes, and he ate everything. Actually Matty has been giving us those great reviews for years. It was really fun. We then cooked for two more whole days, a Saturday and a Sunday. Jennifer Carrillo took all the current pictures throughout. My daughter Emmie and my wife, Tracy, helped out, doing dishes and pots and just by being part of it. We had another day of cooking for the desserts. I really liked that day. Hilda and BT were amazing, and I thank everybody for their hard work and support.

As we said, we made everything in the book. That's a lot of cooking and chopping and peeling and washing. Here's a little tip: clean up as you go along and you'll be done when you're done. Making that much food also proved, happily, how great this food freezes and works as leftovers. My brother, Matty, said he had a different dish every night that week. The chicken soup we froze in four separate Tupperware containers, then opened and defrosted one a day. It was delicious. Sometimes the next day things taste better. I even used the last of the soup for a sauce on penne.

To sum it up, I loved doing this book. I hope you, the reader, enjoys it as well and that it will be helpful in your kitchen. *Another reason I am happy we did this book is that I think there is something special about someone I don't know making my mother's lasagna.* So enjoy, make great food, and if there are any leftovers, call my brother.

Marc and Nick and the Old Man watching

FIRST COURSES

DON'T FILL UP
ON THE ANTIPASTO

We never ate a lot of first courses in our family, but there was one first-course family tradition that everyone loved. Happening at most three times a year (Thanksgiving, Christmas, and sometimes New Year's or Easter), it was the Holiday Antipasto.

A collection of different cheeses, olives, cold cuts, tomatoes, onions, artichoke hearts, sardines, and just about anything else that could be served with oil and vinegar was spread out on a bed of lettuce. You took a small plateful and tried not to fill up. Obviously these were big holidays and much of the family was there. And everyone would tell everyone, "Don't fill up on the antipasto!"

This really was something to worry about because in our family it was important that we also be American. That meant we would be having a full turkey dinner after the lasagna, which came after the antipasto. *It was a badge of honor in our family to still be eating at the end of the dinner, but with too much antipasto you would never make it.* It was so hard to stop eating that antipasto and those little plates didn't help because it didn't seem like you were eating that much. You take a spoonful, trying to make sure you get a little of everything. Sprinkle with some salt and pepper. Pour on some oil and vinegar. Grab a piece of bread. Go sit somewhere and be one with your antipasto. Then try not to go back for more. By the way, we are big on leftovers, and there is nothing like a little leftover antipasto with a turkey sandwich. Just remember, Don't fill up on the antipasto.

Marc, filling up on the antipasto

Holiday Antipasto

Romaine lettuce leaves
4 tomatoes
1 red onion
¼ pound salami, thinly sliced
¼ pound ham, thinly sliced
¼ pound capocollo, thinly sliced
¼ pound sopressata, thinly sliced
Any other cold cuts you like,
    such as mortadella or turkey
Mixed olives

Artichoke hearts
Roasted peppers
Whole mushrooms
Parmesan cheese
Mozzarella cheese
Provolone cheese
Anchovies
Extra virgin olive oil
Red wine vinegar
Salt and pepper

Start with a large platter. Tear the romaine leaves into pieces and spread over the platter. (Any type of lettuce—mixed greens, iceberg—is fine.) Make a bed of the greens. Cut the tomatoes into eighths and spread across the lettuce. Cut the red onion into thin slices and spread them as well. Roll up single slices of the cold cuts like cigars and place them on the platter. Add the mixed olives, artichoke hearts, roasted peppers, mushrooms, and anything else you would like. (We get all these items from an Italian market, but more and more supermarkets are carrying them.) Cut the Parmesan, mozzarella, and provolone into chunks and spread them on the platter. Finish by adding the anchovies. Serve with extra virgin olive oil and vinegar and salt and pepper and let people dress their own antipasto. This is a dish you can and should make your own. Pick out what you do and don't like and add what you want. You really can't go wrong.

Serves 6 to 8
(except if my brother, Matty, is there, then it's less)

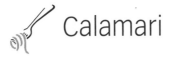 # Calamari

This is a great, fast appetizer. We don't use batter; we just dredge with flour and sauté in garlic and oil. Serve with lemon juice and parsley, or do as we do and make a side sauce for the calamari, which also can be used as a pasta sauce.

Calamari

5 garlic cloves, coarsely chopped
½ cup extra virgin olive oil
1 pound calamari, cleaned and
   cut into rings

1 cup all-purpose flour
¼ cup chopped fresh parsley
Juice of 1 lemon
Salt and pepper

Sauce

1 cup fresh lemon juice
½ cup white wine

½ teaspoon red pepper
Salt and pepper

Sauté the garlic in the olive oil in a large skillet until golden. Remove the garlic to a serving bowl. Dredge the calamari rings and tentacles with the flour and shake off the excess. Sauté the calamari in the olive oil over medium-high heat for about 4 minutes each side and drain on paper towels. Combine the calamari with the garlic. Add the parsley and lemon juice, season with salt and pepper to taste, and serve.

To make the sauce, add the lemon juice, wine, red pepper, and salt and pepper to taste to the same pan. Cook over medium-high heat for 2 minutes, using a wooden spoon to scrape the bottom of the pan and stir. Pour the sauce over the calamari or serve it on the side.

Serves 4 to 6

Bruschetta

This is another appetizer that can get you into trouble. It is so easy to fill up on this dish and that is not by accident. In our family and other Italian families, bruschetta is known as "peasant food." In the Old Country, and when our family first came to America, it was a dish that stretched bread and tomatoes into a meal. Now it is a delicious appetizer that's easy to make.

4 tomatoes, coarsely chopped
1 red onion, chopped
6 garlic cloves, finely chopped
¼ cup chopped fresh basil

Extra virgin olive oil
Balsamic vinegar
Salt and pepper
1 baguette

Mix the tomatoes, onion, garlic, and basil in a large bowl. Add the olive oil, vinegar, and salt and pepper to taste and toss well to coat the tomatoes thoroughly. Cut a baguette in half lengthwise and toast. Cut the toasted bread crosswise into strips. Spoon the tomato mixture onto the bread and serve. This tomato mixture also works well on top of chicken or veal scaloppine.

Serves 4

WHEN GUYS GATHER

My son has a story to tell. He thinks it is soooo funny. I think it is sort of funny, but I do know it is one of the greatest moments in both of our lives. Take it away, Marc.

Thanks, Dad. I love this picture of me and my father because you can really see the emotion on both our faces. To give you a little backstory, it was November 2006 when my wife came to me and told me she was going to have a baby. I was so excited I wanted to call everyone and I did, except my father. I had already done a couple of segments on my father's talk show and had another appearance planned after the New Year, so I decided with my wife (it was really her idea) that we both would tell our parents at the same time on live TV. Julie and I were the only couple from her family that had not had a child yet, so we were getting pressure and a lot of questions like, "Hey, are you gonna give us a grandkid or what?" Julie's parents are Italian too, so they get right to the point.

I'll take it from here, Marc. This picture is taken from a tape of my talk show. *My son was on the show to do a tailgate cooking segment. He can cook anywhere.* In the middle of the segment, all of a sudden he stops and proposes a toast. In the toast he tells me he's going to be a dad and I am going to be a grandpa. This was live, on TV. Try doing the rest of the show. It was not easy. Here's another picture of the little guy.

Marc's Super Bowl Guacamole

8 ripe avocados, pitted, peeled,
  and smashed
3 plum tomatoes, chopped
½ red or white onion, chopped
3 garlic cloves, finely chopped
1½ jalapeño peppers, seeded and
  finely chopped

Juice of ½ lemon and ½ lime
Hot sauce (I like Cholula but
  any hot sauce will do)
Pinch of paprika
Salt and pepper

We smash the avocados with a fork—if you like it chunky, don't smash them as much—then mix in the tomatoes, onion, garlic, and jalapeños. Stir in the lemon and lime juice, a couple of shakes of your favorite hot sauce, the paprika, and salt and pepper to taste. Cover and refrigerate. It's better a couple of hours later.

P.S. This is Marc again. I want to add that I am a HUGE New York Giants fan, and I love to make this every Sunday for the guys that come over to watch the game. Someday when the Giants win the Super Bowl again, I will try to set the world record for the biggest bowl of guacamole and serve it to Giants fans everywhere.

P.P.S. This is Tony. I think my son is nuts.

Serves 8 to 10

CLAMS

Growing up I remember that our family really loved clams. We loved them raw and we loved them in pasta and we loved them in chowder, but we really loved them baked. We actually have a long history with clams. When I think about clams, I always think about my uncle Vinny. He was Aunt Rose's husband, and Rose was my mother's older sister. Vinny was one of my favorite uncles. He was a real character, and I spent a lot of my childhood with him. He lived in Patchogue, out on Long Island. Starting when I was seven, my parents would send me there during the summer to get me out of Brooklyn, because Brooklyn in the summer could be trouble. So for the summer I would live with my aunt and uncle and their two kids. I loved my summers there. My two cousins, Patty and Vivian, took me with them almost everywhere they went, even though I was much younger than they were. And when I wasn't with them, I was with Uncle Vinny. He didn't work as much as my other uncles, so he had a lot of time for me. *To give you an idea of what kind of character he was, he once taught me how to play poker. At the end of the lesson, I owed him fifty*

Uncle Vinny trying
to get a laugh

thousand dollars and my mother's house. Like I said, a real character and so much fun to be with.

Anyway, Uncle Vinny loved clams and he knew how to get them. We would drive to a spot he knew of where we could get to the water very near homes that had seeded their own clam beds. He would send me out into the water with a bushel basket in an inner tube. I would use my feet to dig for the clams. Digging for clams is like doing that old dance the mashed potato. You go from foot to foot digging with the balls of your feet. Then bend over and pick up the clams. Sometimes the homeowners would loudly complain and sometimes the jellyfish were painful, but Uncle Vinny wanted those clams and I was going to get them for him. I would

Uncle Vinny having fun with his daughter, Vivian, and my brother, Matty

actually fill the basket with littlenecks and cherrystones, the smaller ones, the best ones. "No chowders, no big ones," he would say.

The next stop would be the supermarket where Uncle Vinny would "get" a stack of small brown paper bags. He would sometimes use me as a diversion as he "got" them. Then we would sit in the car and put a dozen clams in each bag. The next stop would be the garment factories, where he knew everybody from when he worked there, when he worked. We would sell the clams for two dollars a dozen. He would give me a dollar for my efforts and I felt rich. We would spend days together fishing, clamming, crabbing, and selling. It was paradise for a young kid from Brooklyn, made better by the fact that I had this incredible guide.

I loved my uncle Vinny very much and I learned a lot from him. Some stuff you might not want an uncle to teach a kid, but at least it was always with love. And he, like the rest of the family, showed me something very important. They all had an incredible ability to see the humor in any situation. Even in tragedy they always found the funny. My uncle would say, "That's how you get through life." It is one of their greatest gifts to me and to my son. I know my uncle would have loved my son, Marc. Unfortunately, Marc never got to meet him and that's too, too bad. Marc, of course, has heard all these stories, but retelling them for the book reminded us both of how great Uncle Vinny really was.

UNCLE VINNY'S
CLAM LESSON

If you are going to eat clams, you need to know how to open them. You will need a clam knife, a paring knife, or another good small knife, not a steak knife. For clams on the half-shell or baked clams we like to use the smaller clams, littlenecks or cherrystones. The larger clams are for chowder and soup, and they are called chowders. Place the clams in a colander and give them a real good wash, using a wire brush or the scrub side of a sponge. Then rinse them with cold water. Any that are open should be discarded.

Place the hinge of the clam, the back, against the palm of your hand. Insert the knife blade between the two shells and carefully apply firm pressure with your fingers. Don't wiggle the knife too early or you will break the lip of the shell. Once the knife is in between the shells, work the blade along the top of the shell, cutting the clam loose inside the shell, and open the clam. Cut under the clam on the bottom shell and with the knife move all the clam to the top shell. Twist off the

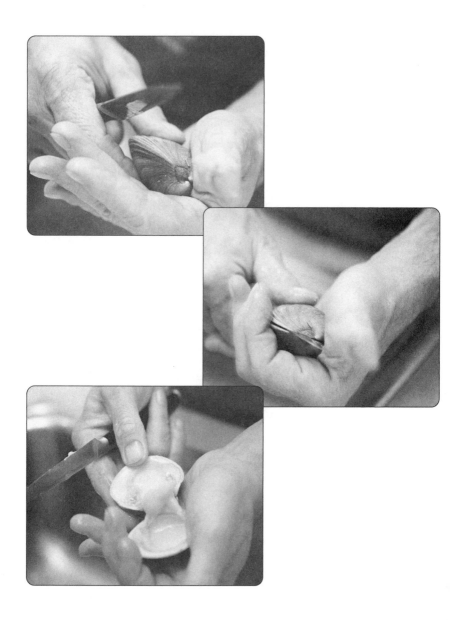

empty shell and discard. (Seems like a lot of work, but you will get better at it.) Now you're ready for some lemon and cocktail sauce.

Uncle Vinny loved clams.

Watch your fingers!

Clams on the Half-Shell

This is not really a recipe, just a way to enjoy the taste of the ocean. This was a family favorite—get the clams open and see how many you can eat. It was like a contest. No matter how many uncles were opening the clams, it was hard to keep pace with the eaters. All you needed on top was a little lemon and maybe some cocktail sauce. Where we lived, on Long Island, there were roadside clam bars. They were always busy. People around there really like their raw clams. You pull over on your way to, or from, the beach and have a dozen. They had the fastest shuckers on the planet. They could open clams as fast as anyone could eat them, well, maybe not my mother. Wash a dozen down with a beer and watch how they do it. Our cocktail sauce was a simple combo of ketchup, horseradish, and lemon. Pretty hard to mess it up.

12 littleneck or cherrystone clams, shucked and on the half-shell

2 tablespoons ketchup
1 teaspoon horseradish
Juice of 1 lemon

Mix the ketchup, horseradish, and lemon juice together. Arrange the clams on a large platter with or without a layer of crushed ice. Serve the sauce alongside.

Serves 4 to 6

UNCLE TONY'S
BAKED CLAMS

Baked clams always remind me of Uncle Tony. That's because when Uncle Tony was around baked clams, you had to eat fast. He was my mother's middle brother. He was married to Aunt Josie and their kids are Johnny, George, and Barbara. I saw a lot of him growing up, and he was around for much of Marc's childhood as well. *He was the quietest of the brothers. He liked Bing Crosby better than Sinatra. He was a prodigious eater.* When the table was set on Sunday, for the macaroni, there would be one setting with a giant salad bowl instead of a normal bowl. That's where Uncle Tony sat.

Once when I was doing a play in New York, my mother told me that my uncle Tony would like to come see the Saturday matinee. I said great and put aside a ticket at the box office in his name. (A little more about my uncle. He was by this time a retired postman. He had come to America from Italy in the twenties with the family and worked hard all his life, but he hadn't seen many plays.) Anyway, he shows up and I get a message that he's there but that he wants to pay for

Uncle Tony and
Aunt Josie

his ticket. No comps for him. I go out and try to argue with him but he has to pay for his ticket. That's the kind of guy he was, and so I let him. We were performing at the Promenade Theatre on the Upper West Side of Manhattan. It is an intimate space and the audience is very close to the stage. The play, *Wrong Turn at Lungfish,* was written and directed by Garry Marshall and is about a blind college professor, a neighborhood girl who volunteers to read to patients at the hospital where he's a patient, and her abusive boyfriend. It's a comedy. I played the boyfriend, the great George C. Scott played the professor, and Jami Gertz played the girl.

In the second act I had a run of my funniest jokes. In the scene I am secretly searching the professor's room while having a conversation with him about opera. Remember, he's blind. The abusive boyfriend actually knows something about opera (I told you it was a comedy). The last place I search is an end table downstage, near the audience. I open the drawer of the table and hear someone in the audience say, "What are you looking for?" Needless to say it stunned me. I was thrown but my big jokes were coming. I got ahold of myself and did my jokes. I actually saw a man in the balcony slap his knee on one of them. With that run over, I had a chance to look into the audience to see who it might have been. Of course, it was my uncle Tony. Hey, I'm his nephew. I was so close, he had to talk to me. The rest of the play went well and the audience stood and cheered.

Backstage in my dressing room I was with a friend when my uncle was brought in by an usher. Trying to make light of the incident, I said to him, "Unc, I am so happy you saw the play, but there is only one rule in the theater, you can't talk to me until after the show's over." He immediately said, "I didn't say anything!" I felt so bad for having automatically blamed him. I said I was sorry, excused myself, and went to use the bathroom. My friend later told me that after about three seconds of awkward silence, my uncle looked at him and said, "I didn't think he heard me."

One last thing about Uncle Tony, when my mom was sick and in the hospital, he would always come and visit her. By that time he had lost his wife, retired, gone back to work, retired again, and was now working delivering food to the elderly. He was an amazing guy. One day, while visiting at the hospital, he was feeling exceptionally well. You see, he was in his seventies, but at that time in his life, he had a girlfriend who was in her thirties. She had a mustache, but that was another story—she was in her thirties. He was sitting across from me with his hands clasped behind his head. He caught my eye, smiled, and made his biceps bounce. He was feeling pretty good.

Baked Clams

24 littleneck or cherrystone clams	½ teaspoon dried oregano
1 cup seasoned dried bread crumbs	Salt and pepper
6 garlic cloves, finely chopped	¼ cup extra virgin olive oil, or as needed
½ cup grated Parmesan cheese	¾ cup water
½ teaspoon red pepper	½ lemon

To make the baked clams that Uncle Tony loved so much, wash the clams well and rinse with cold water. Discard any that are open. Shuck the clams and leave them on the half-shell.

Preheat the oven to 475 degrees or heat the broiler.

Mix the bread crumbs, garlic, Parmesan, red pepper, and the oregano. Season with salt and pepper to taste. Add oil as needed to evenly coat the mixture. Add ¼ cup of the water and mix thoroughly. Spread the mixture on the clams and smooth the edges with a fork or spoon to create a seal.

Place the clams on a baking sheet and drizzle with olive oil. Add the remaining water, about ½ cup, to the pan around the clams.

We use the broiler so these are really broiled, not baked, clams. You can bake them, if you're a stickler, for about 15 minutes, until the bread crumbs are crispy brown. Or broil them on the middle rack for 5 to 7 minutes, until crispy brown. Top with a squeeze of lemon juice and serve.

Serves 4 to 6

SALADS

"GEE, WE HATE TO WASTE A GOOD SALAD"

"Gee, I hate to waste a good salad" is something my father said almost every night after dinner. It was one of those little things that we heard our parents say, or saw them do, as we grew up that stays with us. We all have these memories. As we grow older we think about or say these things, and it reminds us of loved ones and days gone by. For some reason, some of these memories are particularly vivid. "Gee, I hate to waste a good salad" is one of those. The reason my father said this almost every night was because we had a salad almost every night. I think it was my father's attempt to make sure we were getting a healthy diet, a "balanced" diet. *Remember when we all had to have a "balanced" diet?*

Basically we had the same salad almost every night. Occasionally it would have a different ingredient or two, depending on what looked good at the market, but it had its basics. Lettuce. You know, I just had a thought, sometimes that's all it was—lettuce. He used iceberg lettuce. "A head of lettuce," he would say.

Danza Everyday Salad

We use romaine lettuce, although any green leaf works. Tomatoes when they are good. They are great from the garden, and it isn't that difficult to grow a tomato plant. You can actually buy grown tomato plants at some markets and plant them in your yard. Just about anything you like in your salad is fine. Our dressing is olive oil, vinegar (balsamic or red wine), salt and pepper, and a squeeze of lemon over it. Toss well and serve. We know it sounds too simple. It is, but it's a terrific dressing for a salad that goes with just about everything—steak, pasta, fish. One more thing, try dunking your bread in the bottom of the salad bowl. We learned that from Great-grandma.

1 head lettuce, washed and torn into pieces

2 tomatoes, cut into eighths

½ red onion, thinly sliced

1 cucumber, peeled and thinly sliced

1 large garlic clove, finely chopped

¼ cup red wine vinegar

Juice of ½ lemon

½ cup extra virgin olive oil

Salt and pepper

Combine the lettuce, tomatoes, red onion, and cucumber in a large bowl. Mix the garlic, vinegar, and lemon juice in a small jar with a lid or in a small bowl. Add the oil to the jar and shake or gradually add it to the bowl while whisking. Add salt and pepper to taste.

Serves 4 to 6

Arugula, White Bean, and Red Onion Salad

This recipe is a hybrid. It was actually taught to us by Lidia Bastianich, the great Italian chef often seen cooking on her PBS show and the author of many wonderful cookbooks. I was lucky enough to have her on my talk show a few times and once she made this dish. Our family has been making a variation of it for as long as I can remember. It was one of my mother's favorites. We always use canned beans, and Lidia, of course, makes hers from scratch. We also like to toss the beans in garlic and olive oil before putting them in the salad, which Lidia doesn't do in her recipe. Lidia also says any type of bean will do. We like cannellini beans.

2 cans (15 ounces each)
    cannellini beans
2 bunches arugula
1 red onion
4 garlic cloves, finely chopped

½ cup extra virgin olive oil
¼ teaspoon red pepper
Salt and pepper
Juice of 1 lemon

Drain and rinse the cannellini beans in a colander. Pick through the arugula, discarding withered leaves and stems. Wash, pat dry with paper towels, and place in a salad bowl. Thinly slice the red onion and add it to the bowl. Cook the garlic in the olive oil in a large skillet until golden brown. Add the red pepper and a pinch of black pepper to the pan. Add the beans and toss gently in the oil. Remove from the heat and add the beans to the arugula. Season with salt to taste and add the lemon juice. Toss and serve.

Serves 4 to 6

Look at us concentrate.

Marc's Eggplant, Lemon, and Caper Salad

I like this salad on a hot day. It's refreshing and has a little bite. It also has tons of flavor, and people will think you are real fancy if you make it. This recipe is for the vegetarians in the family. My wife used to be a vegetarian until she started eating my father's meatballs, and now she's back eating meat.

1 large eggplant
1 to 2 teaspoons salt
¼ cup extra virgin olive oil
Grated zest and juice of 1 lemon
2 tablespoons capers
15 pitted green Sicilian olives

1 small garlic glove, finely chopped
2 tablespoons chopped fresh parsley
Salt and pepper

Cut the eggplant into 1-inch squares. Place it in a colander and toss the cubes with the salt. Let stand for about 30 minutes, then rinse and pat dry with paper towels.

Heat the oil in a large skillet over medium heat. Add the eggplant and cook, tossing regularly, for about 10 minutes, until golden and softened. Drain the cubes on paper towels and season with salt.

Place the eggplant squares in a large serving bowl and toss with the lemon zest and juice, capers, olives, garlic, and parsley. Season with salt and pepper to taste and serve.

I like to let this dish sit at room temperature for about an hour before serving. That's just me.

Serves 4 to 6

Insalate Tricolore

One of our favorite Italian restaurants in New York City is Patsy's on 56th and 8th in Manhattan. It has been there for over seventy years. Frank Sinatra used to hang out there. The people that run it are dear friends and the food is great. Whenever we go we have Insalate Tricolore. It reminds me of the lettuce-only salad my father made. It is a simple salad of arugula, radicchio, and endive. You can use the all-purpose dressing from our Everyday Salad (page 53) or just use olive oil, lemon juice, salt, and pepper. Use a vegetable peeler to shave a few thin slices of Parmesan and lay the cheese on top of the salad for a great finish.

2 bunches arugula, washed and patted dry
2 heads endive, leaves separated and cut in half
1 head radicchio, washed, patted dry, and cut into strips

½ cup extra virgin olive oil
Juice of 1 lemon
Salt and pepper
Shaved Parmesan cheese

In a salad bowl combine the arugula, endive, and radicchio. Add the olive oil and lemon juice in several batches, tossing the salad each time. Add salt and pepper to taste and toss well. Serve on salad plates and top with shaved Parmesan.

Serves 4 to 6

 # Tony's Caprese Salad

We love buffalo mozzarella (the kind packaged in water) along with a delicious tomato or two. Yellow tomatoes are great and add another color to the salad. Now some basil leaves and optional onion. All right, we have a thing for onions.

1 container (8 ounces)
 mozzarella, packed in water
1 large tomato, sliced
1 onion (optional)

Basil leaves
Salt and pepper
Extra virgin olive oil

Slice the cheese, tomato, and onion, if using, crosswise into ¼-inch-thick rounds. Alternate the slices of cheese, tomato, and onion on salad plates and top with basil. Season with salt and pepper to taste and drizzle with olive oil to finish. We sometimes add a splash of balsamic vinegar as well.

Serves 4 to 6

SOUPS

My father,
out of the Army
after WWII

NOTHING LIKE A NICE
BOWL OF SOUP

As you will see throughout this book, my father was a big influence on me, and because of that, he has also been a big influence on my son, Marc. So many of the things that I say and do come from my father and I, consciously and unconsciously, pass them on to my son. My father had a lot of sayings. Marc's grandfather had a saying for almost everything. One of his favorites was "Two wrongs don't make a right." We heard that a lot growing up.

My father worked as a garbage man for the city of New York, including the street where we lived and the street I went to school on. I was always so proud because he used to drop me off at school with the truck. I'll never forget my first day of high school—he let me ride inside the truck. Just kidding.

My dad would tell me that if I did anything wrong someone in the neighborhood would tell him about it. And that I should remember, and here comes the saying, "One bad thing wipes out all the good you do." That's one way to keep your kids in line. Another one of his favorites was "Finish

strong." To this day I have driven my kids, and myself, crazy with that one. But if you think about it, it's a real good one to live by. We always try to finish strong. When I was young and I would be doing lawn work or the like, and I would complain to my father about how hard the work was, he would say, "That's why they call it work." It didn't help then, but I get it now. So, he loved sayings and clichés. I would say to him, "Dad, that's so cliché," and he would say, "There's a reason it's cliché. A lot of people say it." You couldn't really argue with that.

So, anyway, he also used to say, "There's nothing like a nice bowl of soup." I sort of got what he meant but the word *nice* threw me. I didn't know a bowl of soup could be nice. (Sometimes I thought he was just trying to sell us on the soup. Remember he had to come up with a menu every night.) *Every night! We, my brother and I, were like, "What's for dinner?" Like it was easy.* We never gave him credit for that. At least I didn't, and I wish I had.

Making soup meant that was all he had to do that night. One dish. Not even a salad. Of course, it also meant lots of bread and it was made with lots of love. I learned from my father, and my son learned from me, how nice a bowl of soup can be. So the old man loved soup. We love soup. Our kids love soup. There's nothing like a nice bowl of soup.

My father,
my brother,
and me in
the backyard
in Brooklyn

TIED TO A TREE

We love chicken soup, so we had to be able to make a good one. Chicken soup reminds us of my mother's older sister, Rose. My aunt Rose. She was the other matriarch of the family. She was an extremely beautiful woman, but she wasn't concerned with that. Although when you see a picture of her, you think to yourself, she had to have known how beautiful she was. She had assumed the role of momma's helper early on in life. She was the responsible one. She was the one who cooked, sewed, cleaned, and lived for everyone else. She actually made my mother's, Marc's grandmother's, wedding dress. Unfortunately, she then missed the wedding giving birth to her daughter, our cousin Vivian.

She was tough, real tough, and a real disciplinarian. Once she tied my brother to a tree and beat him with a strap. Not too badly, and he did deserve it. Or am I saying that because he was my younger brother?

Aunt Rose was a great cook. She could and did make everything. Breads, fresh pastas, any dish. She was also a great baker and made many wonderful desserts. She used to send me to get these blackberries from a huge bush around the corner, and she would make a berry pie. I would climb all through that bush eating every other berry. One for Aunt Rose, one for me. I would come back with the telltale signs of blue all over my face. She'd knowingly nod, then send me back for more or simply stretch the berries I hadn't eaten. I had the feeling she was contemplating the strap.

She also made a great chicken soup. She showed me how to make the stock, but it does take a while. My son and I wanted a faster way to make a good chicken soup. So the Danza Boys' Roasted Chicken Soup was born. First you buy a roasted chicken. That's way easier!

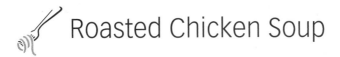

Roasted Chicken Soup

6 quarts water

1 store-bought roasted chicken

1 large onion, peeled and halved

2 tablespoons salt

½ to 1 tablespoon pepper

6 carrots, washed and sliced

6 celery stalks, cleaned and chopped with leaves

1 potato, peeled, halved lengthwise, and thinly sliced

1 small head broccoli, cut into florets

Grated Parmesan cheese

Pour the water into a large pot. Add the chicken, onion, salt, and pepper. Simmer for about 30 minutes, until the chicken is falling apart. Use a spoon to break the chicken apart and continue to simmer. When the broth becomes milky, after about another 30 minutes, strain the soup through a colander. Reserve the broth. Discard the onion and spread the chicken out on a cutting board. Pick out the meat for the soup, discarding everything else. Be careful cleaning the chicken, so you can chew with abandon. Add the chicken to the broth along with the carrots, celery, potato, and broccoli. Bring to a boil, turn off the heat, and let the soup sit for a few minutes. Serve in bowls and top with Parmesan.

P.S. Do not use too much broccoli or it will overwhelm the flavor of the soup. Another option is to leave out the potato and make rice and add a little to each bowl.

Serves 4 to 6

A VERY IMPORTANT UNCLE

Uncle Phil, married to my mother's sister Frances, is a very important uncle. All our uncles were role models, and they all had an incredible work ethic. Except for maybe Uncle Vinny. Again, just kidding. They also all had unique qualities. One of Uncle Phil's was cool. His name is Philly Capasso. He ran a trucking business based in Brooklyn. He drove a flashy car. He has a beautiful wife, our aunt Frances. He wore sharp clothes. He has a pinky ring and a diamond watch. *When he drove us to Brooklyn from his house on Long Island in his Buick*

Uncle Phil with Katie and Emmie at Uncle Matty's wedding

Wildcat, he would thrill us by changing lanes quickly and saying, "You gotta swing out like a cat, man." His booming voice was scary, and when he said to go get the wooden spoon—oh no! He just celebrated his eightieth birthday on the same day my grandson, Nick, turned two. We have been lucky to grow up around him.

One lesson we both always remember Uncle Phil for is his famous, "Follow through. The good guys always follow through." It wasn't just talk—he always practiced what he preached. It's a good lesson, one we should all pass on to our kids. This is his soup. Escarole and beans. We jazzed it up a little and added hot Italian sausage. One night I had no escarole, so I substituted broccolini. I love the way it sounded—broccolini and beans. It tasted great too!

Me and Uncle Phil doing what we do best

LEGENDARY UNCLE

We were going to put this story about Uncle Mike with a recipe but then we remembered he would eat anything. In fact Uncle Vinny once said that Uncle Mike would eat crap out of rusty cup with a bent spoon. Obviously, I cleaned that up.

Anyway, Uncle Mike was legend. My mother's second brother was always the tough guy. When he was a kid, he had more than his share of fights and he was both my mother's protector and my grandfather's enforcer, when she did something wrong. He was big and strong and his feats of strength were retold at many family dinners. He was a World War II veteran and was decorated for bravery and valor. (My father also won a Bronze Star Medal in World War II.) Uncle Mike drove eighteen-wheelers all around the city. He worked for Uncle Philly's company, Jimmyboy Trucking. We lived on Euclid Avenue and would see Uncle Mike bouncing down our street in his huge truck, blowing the air horn for the kids. He was so strong he could pick up and carry a truck transmission. I saw him do it in Uncle Philly's yard on Liberty Avenue. He was also the family handyman. He could fix anything. My mother always had him doing something around our house. I learned how to use a miter box from Uncle Mike. My mother loved wood molding and you use one to match the corners.

My first memory of Uncle Mike was when I was about four or five years old. I was in the backseat of the family car. My mother was driving and it was right after a snowstorm. We had been shopping and were trying to find a parking spot, which was not easy in our neighborhood in Brooklyn, even without the snow. We were under the El on Pitkin Avenue. For those who don't know, the El is an elevated train that runs down the middle of the street. I remember the big nuts and bolts in the supports holding it up. My mom got stuck in the snow. I remember steam and smoke and the windows being all fogged up and my mom was really upset as she tried to rock the car free. All of a sudden out of the smoke came Uncle Mike. He calmed my mother down and lifted the back end of the car and got us out. He probably just pushed the car but in my mind, he picked the car up with one hand and carried us to our parking spot. That's how I remember Uncalo Mike, which is what me and my cousins used to call him.

Another memory of Uncle Mike may not be the most appetizing and not great for a cookbook but it is vivid. I was about eight and we had moved from Pitkin Avenue to Euclid Avenue, the first house my mother and father had ever owned. They were very proud. My mother, of course, was determined to make the house as nice as it could be, so she called Uncle Mike. Like I said, he did everything—carpentry, plumbing, roofing, anything. This one time he was putting linoleum down in our kitchen. When's the last time you heard the word *linoleum*? Uncle Mike had already worked all day and he seemed to be in a hurry. He was using a curved carpet knife that looked like something from the Crusades, and I was watching and trying to help. He was cutting a long piece of the linoleum with the knife when he was distracted by something and just about cut off his index finger. There was a lot of blood and I started to cry. He told me to take it easy and to give him the roll of black electrician's tape in his tool case. I gave him the tape and I asked if we were going to the hospital. He didn't answer. He just bent his finger with his other hand and taped it. He stopped the bleeding with the tape and went back to work. He finished the job and drove himself to the emergency room, where they sewed his finger up. I will never forget his face as he taped his finger to his hand. Blood everywhere, and yet he had this kind of serene look on his face, like he did stuff like this all the time. I could go on about Uncle Mike. There was the time on a hot roof when he drank turpentine thinking it was water. Or the time my cousin Anthony shot Uncle Mike's son, Charles, with a BB gun, and Uncle Mike bent the gun like a carnival strongman. Suffice it to say he was a great influence on me and the rest of the family.

Uncle Mike always used to say, "No moaning no groaning, you have to play the hand you're dealt." That's the way he lived his life, and for us, he was a legendary uncle.

Escarole and Bean Soup

2 heads escarole
6 garlic cloves, coarsely chopped
⅓ cup extra virgin olive oil, plus
    3 tablespoons (optional)
½ teaspoon red pepper
½ teaspoon black pepper
3 cans (15 ounces each) white
    cannellini beans

3 cans (14 ounces each) chicken
    broth
1 teaspoon salt
5 hot or sweet Italian sausages
    (optional)
Grated Parmesan cheese

Discard the brown or wilted leaves from the escarole. Slice off the bottoms, wash the leaves, and tear them in half. Sauté the garlic in ⅓ cup olive oil in a stockpot. Add the red and black pepper. When the garlic is golden, add the cannellini beans. Rinse the cans with about ¼ cup water and add the liquid to the pot. Add the chicken broth and salt and stir. Bring to a boil, then add the cleaned escarole, cover, and remove from the heat.

If you are adding sausage (which we recommend), puncture the sausages all over with a fork. Heat 3 tablespoons oil in a skillet, add the sausages, and brown on all sides for about 8 minutes. Slice the sausages and add to the pot. Bring to a boil and remove from the heat. Serve with Parmesan. And maybe a piece of crusty bread.

Serves 4 to 6

Nothing like a nice bowl of soup

The
Champion
Dukes,
2007

THE DUKES AND HILDA

My son and I play on the same softball team, the Dukes, which has been together for thirty years. I have been there since the beginning, so needless to say, I am one of the older guys still playing. *It's great fun, and as I write this we have a big game tomorrow against the Hitmen. They come by their name honestly.*

But about the soup. The Dukes have traditions. One of them is "Win or lose, we hit the booze," which means we always go out for a beer or something after the game. We often go to a Mexican restaurant on Ventura Boulevard that we really like. Although there are times we have to share it with another team, our archenemy, the Ducky Boys.

I always have a bowl of tortilla soup with my beer. It is not a soup that we grew up with, but we really like it and wanted to learn how to make it. So I asked my Hilda. Hilda has been with our family for nearly thirty years. She's my housekeeper, house manager really. She started cleaning my bachelor pad in the Hollywood Hills in the early eighties. She would come two times a week, Mondays and Fridays, and has been with me ever since. She helped my wife and me raise our two daughters, as she sent her own daughter to UCLA and the University of Wisconsin Law School. Her daughter just graduated with juris doctor's and master's degrees. We are all so proud of her, and I am also proud to say she now works for the city of Madison, Wisconsin, in the Civil Rights Department. My Hilda is a great lady and a great American story, and she cooks too.

That's my Hilda.

Hilda's Tortilla Soup with Chicken and Avocado

1 skinless, boneless whole
    chicken breast, cut in half
3 tablespoons extra virgin
    olive oil
1 yellow onion, very thinly
    sliced
3 garlic cloves, chopped
¼ cup fresh cilantro leaves,
    chopped
1 cup canned plum tomatoes,
    drained

¼ teaspoon ground cumin
4 cups canned chicken broth
Salt and pepper
4½ corn tortillas
½ cup vegetable oil
1 dried New Mexico chile
2½ teaspoons lime juice
1 avocado, peeled, pitted, and
    cut into chunks
¼ cup shredded Monterey Jack
    cheese

Cook the chicken breast in simmering water to cover for about 15 minutes and drain.

Warm 2 tablespoons of the olive oil in a pan over medium heat. Add the onion, garlic, and 2 pinches of the cilantro and cook until the onion softens and begins to turn golden brown, about 10 minutes. Combine this mixture with the tomatoes in a blender and process until smooth.

Warm the remaining tablespoon of olive oil in a large saucepan over medium-high heat. Add the tomato mixture and cumin. Stir the mixture, as you cook, until thick and dark, about 5 minutes. Add the chicken broth. Cover and simmer, stirring occasionally, for about 20 minutes. Cut the chicken into strips, add to the pan, and simmer for about 2 minutes more. Season to taste with salt and pepper.

Cut the tortillas into thin strips. Heat the vegetable oil in a large skillet over medium-high heat. When the oil is hot, drop in the strips and turn them until they are crisp. Transfer to paper towels and drain.

Toast the chile in a dry skillet over medium heat for about 7 minutes, then crumble it, removing the seeds. Ladle the soup into bowls and evenly add the tortilla strips, crumbled chile, remaining cilantro, the lime juice, avocado, and cheese. Serve immediately.

Serves 4 to 6

PATTY

This next soup is like an Italian egg drop soup, easy to make and delicious. It reminds us of our dear cousin Patty. He was Aunt Rose and Uncle Vinny's son. He had a huge influence on me and my son. He was Marc's confirmation sponsor. He was almost six years older than I was, and when I lived with his family during the summers, he took me everywhere with him. I was like his pet. He was a teenager with a car and a girlfriend and I was nine. He affected me in a lot of ways. He taught me how to drive when I was ten, although I couldn't reach the pedals. He introduced me to doo-wop music and I love doo-wop music.

When I was eleven, I got my first real kiss from a girl in the backseat of his friend's car. One day I was sitting on the console between them in a 1961 Oldsmobile. We were cruising around Patchogue, Long Island, leaving rubber. Just then they saw these two girls and asked them if they wanted a ride. The girls said yes and got in the car. I jumped in the backseat and was up against the window trying not to be there. They all started to kid around, and Patty said to the girl between us, who was about seventeen, "Why don't you kiss the kid?" I didn't want to look

Patty was Marc's sponsor at confirmation.

as scared as I was but I couldn't help it. Suddenly she leaned over and kissed me. Then she put her tongue in my mouth and I almost had a heart attack. I can still hear my heart beating out of my chest. They all had a good laugh. Talk about a memory.

Most of all, though, Patty affected us with his love. My son was lucky enough to know him for many years, and we both know it was his heart that was so great. He was, truly, a person that would be there for you, no matter what. When Patty was alive, we used to go to Elaine's, the famous watering hole and restaurant in New York City. We would always have *stracciatella* (egg drop soup)—it was Patty's favorite. When we go there now, we always order a bowl for Patty, even though he's not there to have it.

Cousin Patty
with Katie and
Emily

As I said, my son was also very close to cousin Patty. Your turn, Marc.

I also have many fond memories of Cousin Patty. I feel like I was just really getting to know him in a way when we lost him. One such memory is New Year's Eve 1995. I had just graduated college and gotten myself a job in Rhode Island, working for ESPN. My wife and I decided to drive down to New York City for New Year's Eve. I, of course, immediately called Cousin Patty. You see Patty might well have been the honorary mayor of New York City. He worked for the city, maintaining city buildings, and he knew everybody. He even parked wherever he wanted. Even though he lived out on Long Island, in Lynbrook, Patty went to the "City" every day and night for as long as I could remember. He would make it there so fast you couldn't believe it. That night he took us on a tour of my father's old neighborhood—the East New York section of Brooklyn, which, by the way, had changed some. It's a really tough place now. Then we went to Times Square for the ball drop. On the way he waved and yelled at people while singing completely out of sync and tune with Meat Loaf, blaring out of his stereo. We ate, drank, and enjoyed the greatest city in the world together. There will never be anyone like him. *He made happy noises when he ate and had plenty of stains on his shirt.* When he laughed, he wheezed this jolly belly noise that was infectious. He was tough on things: cars, couches, chairs, remote controls, you name it. He was a kid at heart and would do anything for you. That's the way he lived and that's why we miss him so.

Patty's Italian Egg Drop Soup

3 cans (14 ounces each) chicken broth
Salt and pepper
3 cups fresh spinach, washed and cut into strips

3 eggs, beaten
3 tablespoons milk
½ cup grated Parmesan cheese

Bring the chicken broth to a boil in a large pan and season with salt and pepper to taste. Stir in the spinach and cook until wilted, about 1 minute. Beat the eggs with the milk and drizzle them into the soup while stirring, breaking the eggs into ribbons. The eggs cook fast, about as long as it takes to put them in. Remove from the heat. Serve the soup in bowls and top with Parmesan.

Serves 4 to 6

PIZZA

Me and my grandmother on her eighty-fifth birthday

YOU GONNA EAT THAT LAST PIECE OF PIZZA?

My mother's side of the family is Sicilian; my father's side, Neapolitan, or from Naples. There were always comparisons and things that were supposedly unique to each region. It was almost a competition. For instance, my mother said that a Sicilian never takes the last one of anything. By the way, we haven't mentioned this before: my mother's family came from Campobello di Mazara, in Sicily. It is a small town near Marsala, which is on the southwest coast of the island. They left Sicily in 1929, my grandfather, grandmother, and their six children. They arrived here, in America, just in time for the Depression. Good timing. They settled in Brooklyn, New York, where they had relatives.

Anyway, about not taking the last one. Growing up, I remember there was always "one" left. One meatball. One sausage. One. One left. You knew someone wanted it. Someone would eat it just for the hell of it, but there it was. All by itself. *They fed all those people, and they happened to make one meatball more than just enough.* This rule applied to everything.

To this day I don't take the last one. Well, at least not while anyone is looking.

Of course, this applied to pizza. The first time I was aware of the "Don't take the last piece" rule was when my grandmother, Marc's great-grandmother, made pizzas. Notice the plural. As we said, Grandma lived with us, and when she made pizzas it was like a national holiday. She didn't do it that often as it was a lot of work, she had to make so many pies. The funny thing was that there was no announcement that she was making pizzas, but everyone would start to show up. All the cousins, uncles, aunts. Even the people you called uncle and aunt that weren't really your uncle and aunt, they came too. Grandma made a deep-dish Sicilian pie with a great crust and more than a pinch of oregano. I can still remember how great it smelled and tasted. She didn't have a pizza oven or even a pizza stone, but somehow she made a great homemade pizza.

The big difference between ours and hers is that we make a thin crust and don't use that much oregano. We think a little oregano goes a long way. We do use a pizza stone and we like the ¾-inch thickness. You can get them at just about every housewares store. But one thing is the same—the dough. I can remember watching my grandmother kneading the dough. Covered in flour, she would work each piece hard, rolling it and folding it in on itself. She would give me a small piece to make my own little pizza. I have done that with all three of my kids. I give them a little ball of dough, and then we have a flour fight. It's fun to watch them trying to mimic me but also making it their own.

Marc was lucky to be around his great-grandmother, and here's how he remembers it:

I got to try Great-grandma's pizza one time before she passed, and I still remember how good it was, even though it was very different from the pizza my father cooks these days. That was twenty-seven years ago but the taste and smell have stayed with me. It's the one real memory I have of my great-grandmother cooking. If I close my eyes, I can taste and smell that pizza in Aunt Rose's backyard and see my great-grandmother smiling at the kids over a little glass of red wine. She was a round, short woman who loved to pinch cheeks, give great big hugs, and whisper "kookookidikoo" in your ear. Hey, how many guys can say they ate their great-grandmother's pizza?

Pizza night in the backyard
Left to right:
Phyllis, Geri, Grandma, Uncle Tony, and Uncle Mike

"Dough" boys

Pizza Dough

1 package fast-rising yeast
1 cup warm water
1 teaspoon sugar
3½ cups all-purpose flour

1 tablespoon salt
1 tablespoon plus 2 teaspoons
   extra virgin olive oil
1 tablespoon honey (optional)

We make pizza dough by first proofing the yeast. (Gee, I love that kind of talk.) Here's how you do it: Stir the yeast, ½ cup of the warm water, and the sugar together in a mixing bowl. Let stand for 10 minutes. Put the flour in another mixing bowl. Make a well in the flour and add the salt and 1 table-spoon oil. Sometimes I add 1 tablespoon honey because I like the added hint of sweetness. Add about half the yeast mixture and blend. Add the rest of the yeast and the rest of the warm water as needed to get it all to stick together.

Take the dough out of the bowl, place on a floured board or counter, and knead for 7 to 10 minutes, until smooth and elastic. Cut the dough in half and round off each half by folding the dough onto itself with your fingers. (Got that tip from a real pizza maker.) Place each ball of dough in a soup

bowl with 1 teaspoon oil. Turn and coat the dough with the oil. Cover with plastic wrap and let it rise about 2 hours, until double in size.

Makes dough for 2 pizzas

Look at
that arm!

The Rest of the Pie

This recipe makes two pizzas.

Cornmeal
Pizza Dough (page 97)
Extra virgin olive oil
½ cup tomato sauce (Quick or
Date Sauce is great for
pizza, page 113)

1 cup grated Parmesan cheese
1 package (8 ounces)
mozzarella cheese, cut into
1-inch pieces
Salt and pepper
Shredded fresh or dried basil
leaves

Preheat the oven with a pizza stone on the middle rack to
550 degrees for 30 minutes, then reduce the temperature to
500 degrees.

You will need a pizza peel or a cookie sheet. Sprinkle cornmeal liberally on the peel. This will help the pizza slide off the
peel and onto the stone.

Take one ball of dough and stretch or roll it into a flat circle.
Using your fingers, form a ridge around the outside. Slide the

dough onto the peel. If you shake the peel, the pizza should slide back and forth.

Spread ¼ cup of the tomato sauce, more if you need it, right up to the outer ridge. Spread half of the Parmesan and mozzarella over the sauce.

To place the pizza on the stone, pull out the oven rack and place pizza peel on the stone. Shake the peel and get the pizza moving, then tilt the peel as you shake. When the pizza hits the stone, slide the peel out, leaving the pizza on the stone.

Success!

Bake for 10 to 15 minutes, spinning it occasionally. It should be golden brown underneath. We like it a bit well done. Keep an eye on it. When cooked, slide the pizza back onto the peel, then slide it onto a platter. Add salt and pepper to taste and spread basil leaves all over. Let cool for 1 or 2 minutes before serving.

While the first pizza bakes, repeat with the second ball of dough and the remaining ingredients to make the second pizza.

Serves 6 to 8

The most
beautiful girl in
the world—my
mother's mother,
Anna Camisa

Grandma's Sicilian Pizza

This is Grandma's pizza, made with a thick crust and lots of oregano. She lined a large baking pan with her dough, making an even layer, then she would brush it with olive oil. There would be small puddles of oil in the indentations her fingers made in the dough.

Extra virgin olive oil
Pizza Dough (page 97)
½ teaspoon dried oregano
Quick or Date Sauce
  (page 113)
1 cup grated Parmesan cheese

1 package (8 ounces)
  mozzarella cheese, cut into
  1-inch pieces
Fresh basil leaves, shredded
Salt and pepper

Preheat the oven to 500 degrees.

Lightly oil a large baking pan (13 x 9 x 2 will do). Spread all the dough across the bottom of the pan and an inch or so up the sides. You want to create a "deep" thick crust. Brush the dough with oil.

Add the oregano to the sauce (more if you like, but remember a little goes a long way) and simmer for 5 minutes. Cover the entire surface of the dough with a thin or thick layer of sauce. Spread the Parmesan, mozzarella, and basil over top. Bake for about 20 minutes. It should be crispy. Let stand a few minutes before removing it from the pan. You can sprinkle it with more oregano and add salt and pepper to taste.

Serves 4 to 6

Little Nick
Danger

PASTA

Grandma, Aunt Fran, and Aunt Sadie in Brooklyn a long time ago

Aunt Frances and her mother

TWO MINUTES

In our house "two minutes" was the answer to any question about when something would be ready.

"Is the macaroni ready?"

"Two minutes."

"When are we eating?"

"Two minutes."

"Coffee?"

"Two minutes."

But when it came to the macaroni, the pasta, two minutes could be the difference between great and very, very bad. It was important the pasta be al dente, or not soft. There is an art to getting it right. *Too soon, too hard; too late, too soft.*

Pasta was a big part of our lives. When I was a kid, I think we ate macaroni three times a week. One of the best macaroni makers, even though she didn't eat it, was our aunt Frances, my mother's younger sister. She never ate pasta, and in our family that was odd. She's a classic lady and an inspiration. She has overcome many hardships but always has a smile and some sweet advice for me. She's smart, funny, and she's great, singing along with me and my ukulele. As you can see

Our sweet
aunt Frances

by the picture, she was the glamorous one in the family, but her real beauty is in her heart. She has in some ways taken my mother's place for me, and I love her so for that.

Aunt Frances's method for making perfect pasta is to keep a close eye on it. Bring the water to a boil. Add a couple of tablespoons of salt. Bring it back to a boil and put in your pasta. It has to be hot, so leave it covered until it starts to boil again. Stir to make sure nothing is sticking to the pot. In about 7 or 8 minutes it should be close. Take a piece out and try it. It should not be hard but still firm. It should also be how you like it. It may take a few tries to get it just right, but as Aunt Frances used to say, "My money's on you."

Bolognese Sauce with Spaghetti

This is a recipe we have been making only for the past few years. It is not something we grew up with, but Marc and I love it and the kids really like it too. It doesn't take long to make and it's really delicious. We like to spice it up with red pepper flakes.

1 can (35 ounces) plum
   tomatoes with basil
¼ cup extra virgin olive oil
1 small to medium onion,
   chopped
2 garlic cloves, finely chopped
1 celery stalk, chopped
1 carrot, chopped
1 pound ground beef

½ cup fresh parsley leaves,
   chopped
¼ cup fresh basil leaves, chopped
¼ to ½ teaspoon red pepper
   flakes (optional)
Salt and pepper
1 pound spaghetti
¼ cup freshly grated Parmesan
   cheese

Strain the tomatoes in a colander to extract the juice, breaking apart the tomatoes with your fingers. Discard the pulp. Heat the olive oil in a large skillet. Add the onion and garlic and sauté over medium heat until the onion becomes soft, about 3 minutes. Add the celery and carrot and sauté for another 5 minutes. Add the ground beef and sauté, breaking up any large lumps with a wooden spoon, for about 9 minutes, until the meat is browned all over. Add the tomatoes, parsley, and basil and cook over medium heat until the sauce thickens, about 10 minutes. If you are using it, add the red pepper, then season with salt and pepper to taste.

Prepare the pasta as usual (page 110). We use spaghetti for this, but any pasta you like is fine. Cook the pasta al dente, drain, and toss with the sauce. Serve in bowls and top with Parmesan.

Serves 4 to 6

 # Quick or Date Sauce

This was my date sauce. My son and I have both used this sauce to impress. Women love men who cook, and if the food tastes great, you will be a hero. Get the picture? It's an easy recipe. It's quick but it will make you look like a gourmet who knows his or her way around the kitchen.

1 can (35 ounces) plum
   tomatoes with basil
½ cup water
3 tablespoons extra virgin
   olive oil
1 medium onion, chopped
2 garlic cloves, chopped

¼ teaspoon red pepper
½ cup red wine
2 tablespoons tomato paste
1 teaspoon salt
¼ teaspoon black pepper
½ cup chopped fresh basil

Strain the plum tomatoes in a colander to extract the juice, breaking apart the tomatoes with your fingers. Discard the pulp. Rinse the can with ½ cup water and add it to the juice. Warm the oil in a saucepan over medium heat. Add the onion, garlic, and red pepper and sauté until the onion becomes slightly brown, about 4 minutes. Add the tomatoes, wine, tomato paste, salt, and black pepper. Bring to a boil, then reduce the heat and simmer for 25 minutes. Add the basil and simmer for 5 minutes more.

P.S. To serve, bring 1 pound of pasta (your choice) to a boil and cook until al dente. Drain the pasta, put it back in the pot, and add 1 cup of the sauce. Cook for 1 minute over high heat to let the pasta absorb the flavor of the sauce. Mix in the remaining sauce and serve.

Serves 4 to 6

My son is the cool one with the shades.

Sherman Oaks Pesto with Fusilli and Chicken

This is an example of my son's creative cooking. Take it away, son.

Sure, Dad. This is different than a regular pesto. My wife and I like spicy food, and I cook a lot with jalapeños, so I figured, let's try it in pesto! This turned out to be such a good recipe that I cooked it on my father's talk show, and I can tell you that the production crew ate it all after the segment. Every bit of it. That made me feel great. This pesto can be used in so many ways, and you will have enough for other dishes. Try it on fish, salad, chicken, or pasta. It can be served hot or cold. Let it sit overnight in the refrigerator. It's always better the next day.

Pesto

2 fresh jalapeño peppers
   (one green, one red), seeded
1 tablespoon sugar
1 tablespoon minced ginger
1 cup macadamia nuts
Grated zest of 2 lemons

1 whole head garlic, cloves peeled
1 cup extra virgin olive oil
½ cup fresh mint leaves
1 cup fresh basil leaves
½ cup fresh cilantro leaves
Salt and pepper

2 teaspoons Lawry's seasoned
  salt
1 tablespoon Worcestershire
  sauce
1 teaspoon soy sauce

2 boneless, skinless whole
  chicken breasts, halved
1 pound fusilli
½ cup extra virgin olive oil
2 cups cherry tomatoes, halved

For the pesto, blend the jalapeños, sugar, ginger, macadamia nuts, lemon zest, garlic, and ½ cup of the olive oil in a food processor. Add the herbs and slowly pour in the remaining ½ cup of the oil while the machine is running. Process until a puree is formed. Season with salt and pepper to taste.

To prepare the chicken, mix the seasoned salt, Worcestershire, and soy sauce in a shallow bowl. Add the chicken and turn to coat. Marinate for 20 minutes, turning once or twice.

Preheat the oven to 350 degrees.

Remove the chicken from the marinade and put it in a large casserole. Cover with foil and bake for 15 to 20 minutes.

To make the pasta, bring a large pot of salted water to a boil and cook the fusilli until al dente.

Add the ½ cup of olive oil to a large skillet and heat to smoking. Cut the cooked chicken into chunks or julienne and sear in the hot olive oil. Remove and drain on paper towels.

Drain the pasta and transfer to a large bowl. Add the chicken and tomatoes, then toss with enough pesto to coat but not to drench it.

Serves 4 to 6

Uncle John
and
Aunt Rose
in Bristol,
Pennsylvania

UNCLE JOHN

My uncle John, Mr. John Camisa, was my mother's oldest brother and they were very close. I can still hear her saying "Oh, my brother John, my brother John." He was married to our aunt Anne, and she was one of the "Lee sisters," which was the name my uncle had given to his wife and her two sisters, Jean and Ella. He would say, "Here they are—the Lee sisters, Ugly, Beastly, and Ghastly." It wasn't an insult to them, though, far from it. Once, I heard my Aunt Anne say, after she was introduced as Ghastly, "No, John, I'm Beastly. She's Ghastly," pointing to her sister Ella.

My uncle and I were close and became even more so after my mother passed away. We talked on the phone almost every day, and he became a sort of surrogate father to me. He was a very good influence on me during some tumultuous times. He was an old-fashioned guy, smart and straightforward with an easy smile. When he died I flew in from Los Angeles for his funeral. Luckily I had seen him just a few weeks before, and I was so grateful for that. At the cemetery I was very emotional and cried into a handful of tissues. I put those tissues into the pocket of my coat. Now, this coat I only wore in cold weather, which means I normally wear it only when I am on the East Coast. Almost a year later, wearing that coat again, I reached into the pocket and pulled out this handful of crumpled tissues. I was staring at them when my wife asked me what I was looking at. I thought for a moment and said, "It's Uncle John's tears."

Uncle John's Pasta with Prosciutto Sauce

1 tablespoon extra virgin
   olive oil
4 garlic cloves, chopped
1 medium onion, chopped
½ head celery, chopped
1 can (14 ounces) chicken broth

¼ teaspoon red pepper
¼ teaspoon black pepper
½ teaspoon salt
½ pound prosciutto, coarsely
   chopped
1 pound pasta

Heat the oil in a large skillet over medium-high heat. Add the garlic, onion, and celery and sauté until soft, 4 to 5 minutes. Add the broth, red and black pepper, and the salt and bring to a simmer. Add the prosciutto and simmer for 5 minutes.

Meanwhile cook the pasta in a large pot of boiling salted water until al dente. While the pasta is cooking, take 1 cup of the starch water from the pasta pot and add it to the sauce. Continue to simmer the sauce for another 2 minutes. Drain the pasta and combine it with the sauce.

Serves 4 to 6

Dinner
at Aunt
Rose's

SUNDAY SAUCE

It's wonderful to grow up in a large extended family with lots of uncles, aunts, and older and younger cousins. My son and I were lucky to have that. My mother's family did more than keep in touch, they lived near each other. In about a five-block radius, we had four sets of aunts and uncles with their children, and my grandma and grandpa too. That guaranteed a full house for Sunday dinner. That meant a big dinner with a big kids' table, and that also meant Sunday sauce.

Sunday sauce was different. First, there was more of it. It was a big sauce in a big pot, and there were a lot of things in it. When my grandfather was alive, you never knew what might end up in the sauce. He liked rabbit and some other stuff he wouldn't tell the kids about. Second, it cooked a long time. No shortcuts on Sunday.

It was fun when everybody was there. My mother's brothers Mike and Tony would kid with my aunt Rose's husband, Vinny. My father and Uncle Phil kidded all the aunts. Uncle Tony lifting me over his head with one hand. All the cousins running around. The Italian and English all mixed up. The

Pick up your head. (Emmie)

neighbors stopping by. The moans and groans when everyone had to leave. Family.

Nowadays my son and I keep up the family Sunday tradition at one or the other of our houses. Most of the time we have it at my house, but we have made it over to his. He and his wife have a great house, right around the corner from our house. That's another tradition we try to keep alive—living close together. Making up the rest of the regular group are Marc's wife (Julie) and their son (Nicholas), my brother (Matty) and his wife (Jackie), my wife (Tracy) and our two daughters (Emily and Katie—although now Katie is away at

Everybody works. (Katie)

school), and any of our friends who are nearby and hungry. As they used to say when we were kids, "More company! Throw another pound of macaroni in the pot." What they made then, and what we make now, is the Sunday sauce. It always has meatballs and pork ribs, and sometimes has braciole and/or sausages. Obviously this is a meat sauce. Not gravy. We think gravy goes on turkey.

We start them
young! (Nick)

Sunday Sauce
with Meatballs

Sauce

2 cans (35 ounces each) plum
    tomatoes with basil
¼ cup extra virgin olive oil
4 garlic cloves, chopped
1 medium onion, chopped
½ teaspoon black pepper
¼ teaspoon red pepper flakes

½ cup red wine
½ cup grated Parmesan cheese ?
1 teaspoon salt
1 cup water
½ cup fresh basil leaves, cut into
    thin strips

Meatballs and Ribs

↓ OR ¼ CUP.

1 pound ground sirloin or lean
    ground beef, pork, turkey, veal,
    chicken, or any combination
2 eggs
6 garlic cloves, finely chopped
    OR "POWDER
½ cup seasoned bread crumbs
1 tablespoon salt
1 teaspoon black pepper

✗ ½ cup grated Parmesan cheese
½ cup milk ?
1 cup all-purpose flour   *Sauté*
1 cup extra virgin olive oil   *Onion in*
3 garlic cloves, chopped   *the oil*
1 pound pork spareribs, trimmed *when*
1 can (6 ounces) tomato paste *frying*

the flour-coated
        meatballs
asoda combine in
tomato sauce, sausage,
+ pepperoni + simmer

127

Making meatballs

In our family we use San Marzano plum tomatoes with basil. Strain the tomatoes in a colander to extract the juice, breaking the tomatoes apart with your hands. Discard the pulp. (This eliminates the bitter part of the tomato.)

Next make the meatballs. Put the ground meat in a mixing bowl. Beat the eggs and add them to the meat along with 6 cloves garlic, the bread crumbs, salt, pepper, Parmesan, and milk. Mix this all together with your hands. Wet your hands with water and continue to wet them as you pinch meat from the bowl and roll into 2-inch balls. Roll the balls in the flour.

Heat the oil in a large skillet. Add 3 cloves chopped garlic and sauté until golden brown. Remove the garlic with a slotted spoon and set aside. Add the meatballs and sauté over medium-high heat, turning them, until they are brown all over. As soon as you can pick them up with a fork, they are ready. You don't want them to be well done. (If the meatball slides off the fork when you pick it up, it needs to cook a little longer.)

Cut the ribs apart. Sauté them in the hot oil until very brown and remove. Return the garlic to the oil and add the tomato paste to the pan. Cook, stirring, over medium heat for about 3 minutes. Remove from the heat.

Back to the sauce: Heat the olive oil in a large pot over medium-high heat. Add 4 cloves garlic, the onion, red and black pepper and sauté until the onion is soft and beginning to brown, about 5 minutes. Add the juiced tomatoes, red wine, Parmesan, and salt. Add the tomato paste and the water and stir together over medium heat. Add the meatballs and spareribs. Bring to an easy boil, then simmer over low heat for 2 hours.

Add the basil and simmer for 15 minutes more. The spareribs should be very tender, falling off the bone, and the meatballs should float in the sauce.

Serves 4 to 6

Don't be afraid—
I won't wreck!

DON'T BE AFRAID

When I first started cooking with my father, he would stand over me and tell me how to do things. But let's have my son, Marc, talk about cooking with me. You're on, Marc.

My father taught me many important lessons in life. One lesson that sticks out applies to more than just cooking. He would say in a deep voice as he stood over the stove, "Don't be afraid," and drop more garlic into the pan or add more salt. When he was cooking, that statement applied to the ingredients, as in "don't be afraid" to add more, but he also taught me this about success and failure: You can't be afraid of either.

When my father cooked dinner, he always made at least three things—an entrée and a salad were a given—it was that side dish that was an issue at times. I remember him saying, "I have to come up with another something." Then from out of nowhere he would whip something up like sautéed broccoli in oil and garlic or fried potatoes with onions. He would rumble through the cupboards and refrigerator mumbling and grunting. My father is constantly making noise when he cooks. He would never win a silent cook-off. When he takes pans out, it undoubtedly sounds like a huge car wreck. But most of the time you come in the kitchen and find him singing. It's really a stage for my father, and it's so fun to watch him and be a part of it.

Roasted Vegetable Pasta

8 garlic cloves, chopped
¼ cup extra virgin olive oil
¼ cup chicken broth
2 tablespoons fresh thyme leaves
1 teaspoon salt
Pepper
3 heirloom or plum tomatoes,
   cut into fourths

1½ pounds zucchini, thinly sliced
1 red onion, thickly sliced
½ cup black olives, pitted and
   coarsely chopped
1 pound penne
⅓ cup flat-leaf parsley leaves,
   chopped
Grated Parmesan cheese

Preheat the oven to 375 degrees.

Place the garlic in a shallow roasting pan and drizzle with the oil and broth. Sprinkle with the thyme, the salt, and pepper to taste. Cover with foil and bake for 30 minutes.

Add the tomatoes, zucchini, onion, and olives to the garlic. Bake, uncovered, for 45 minutes, until the vegetables are tender, tossing the vegetables once or twice.

Meanwhile, cook the pasta in a large pot of boiling salted water until al dente and drain.

Remove the vegetables from the oven and adjust the seasonings. Toss with the parsley and cooked pasta in a large bowl. Serve hot or at room temperature with Parmesan.

Serves 4 to 6

Pasta with Garlic and Oil

This is one of our favorites and another example of what they used to call "peasant food." It's so easy. We make it often for my brother's wife. My sister-in-law, Jackie, is a vegetarian, a strict one, who loves pasta with garlic and oil. So on Sunday, when we are happily eating meatballs, she's happy as well. A small portion makes a great first course for us carnivores.

1 pound pasta
Salt
6 tablespoons extra virgin
    olive oil
6 garlic cloves, coarsely chopped
¼ teaspoon red pepper

¼ teaspoon freshly ground black
    pepper
¼ cup fresh parsley leaves,
    chopped
Grated Parmesan cheese

Start by boiling water for the pasta in a large pot. Add 2 table-spoons salt and bring it back to a boil. Stir in whatever pasta you want, any type works.

Heat 4 tablespoons of the oil in a large skillet over medium heat. Add the garlic and cook until golden brown. Remove from the heat and add the red and black pepper. Stir in ½ cup of the starch water from the pasta pot. Add the remaining 2 tablespoons oil, the parsley, and salt to taste. Drain the pasta and toss with the sauce. Serve with grated Parmesan.

P.S. The next day sauté the leftover pasta over medium heat. It makes a great side dish or appetizer.

Serves 4 to 6

Pasta Nicky

Here's another of Marc's original recipes. Tell us about it, son.

This is a great pasta I came up with to get my son, Nicholas, to eat carrots and peas. It's a colorful pasta that tastes great and is extremely light and easy and healthful. For some reason I had a lot of trouble getting Nick to eat carrots, but he needs that vitamin A. I used to give him peas when he was a baby but he wouldn't eat them. Usually he just threw them all over the floor. As he got older, I had to come up with ways to get him to eat his veggies. This pasta seems to be a winner. He loves it, and I am so happy because he's finally eating carrots!

½ cup extra virgin olive oil
1 tablespoon butter
4 garlic cloves, chopped
½ onion, thinly sliced
3 carrots, peeled and chopped

1 cup frozen green peas
1 teaspoon salt
Pepper
Pinch of sugar
1 pound bow-tie pasta

Heat the oil, butter, and garlic in a large skillet over medium heat until the butter melts and the oil becomes hot. Add the

What a face—
face *bello*!

onion, carrots, and peas and cook until the vegetables begin to soften. Season with the salt and pepper to taste and add the sugar. Cover and simmer for 15 minutes, stirring occasionally.

Meanwhile cook the pasta in a large pot of boiling salted water until al dente, 7 to 8 minutes. Drain the pasta, combine with the vegetables, and serve.

Serves 4 to 6

One of those
summers
on Long
Island—
me and Patty
with our
shirts off

THE GIANT
OF PATCHOGUE

I remember being in Patchogue at Aunt Rose and Uncle
Vinny's house one day when I was about eleven years old.
Most of the family was there, and the adults were planning
dinner. My uncles and my father went to get some seafood.
They came back, about an hour later, with the biggest lobster
I have ever seen. I was young and everything looked big to
me, but this was a monster. Uncle Mike chased all the kids
with it. We screamed and ran around the yard. Then he took
a Popsicle stick and put it in the lobster's claw. The lobster
broke it. Then the kids really screamed. This lobster was so
big that it had to have been at least forty years old, and it
wasn't the most tender, so it went right into a sauce. This next
recipe doesn't have lobster in it, but for some reason it makes
me think of the Giant Lobster of Patchogue.

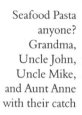

Seafood Pasta
anyone?
Grandma,
Uncle John,
Uncle Mike,
and Aunt Anne
with their catch

 # Seafood Pasta

This is a great recipe and really not that hard to make. You can use any type of fish or shellfish, even lobster if you want.

1 can (35 ounces) plum
    tomatoes with basil
1 cup water
2 tablespoons extra virgin olive oil
4 garlic cloves, chopped
½ cup dry white wine
½ pound cleaned calamari, cut
    into rings
¼ teaspoon red pepper
Salt and freshly ground black
    pepper
1 white-fleshed fish fillet (about

6 to 8 ounces), such as cod,
    perch, or halibut, skinned
    and cut into large chunks
½ pound shrimp, shelled and
    deveined
12 littleneck clams, scrubbed
12 mussels, debearded and
    scrubbed
¼ cup fresh basil leaves, chopped
¼ cup fresh parsley leaves,
    chopped
1 pound pasta

Strain the tomatoes in a colander using your hands to break apart the tomatoes to extract the juice. Discard the pulp. Rinse the can with 1 cup water and add it to the tomato juice. Heat the oil in a large saucepan over medium heat. Add the garlic and sauté until golden brown. (And yes, we do realize that almost all of our recipes start this way.) Add the tomato juice, wine, calamari, red pepper, and salt and pepper to taste. Bring to a boil, then reduce the heat and cover. Simmer for 25 minutes.

Add the fish, shrimp, clams, and mussels to the sauce. Increase the heat to medium, cover the pan, and cook for 10 minutes. The clam and mussel shells will open (any that don't should be discarded). Stir in the basil and parsley and cook for 5 minutes more. Season with salt and pepper to taste.

Meanwhile cook the pasta in a large pot of boiling salted water until al dente. Drain and place in a serving bowl. Spoon the sauce and seafood over the pasta, toss, and serve.

Serves 4 to 6

Holiday Antipasto (page 23)

Roasted Chicken Soup (page 71)

Pasta with Fresh Tomatoes, Arugula,
and Clams (page 148)

Marc's Tangerine-Honey Chicken
with Chipotle Glaze (page 196)

Sherman Oaks Pesto with Fusilli
and Chicken (page 115)

Pasta and Sunday Sauce with Meatballs (page 127)

Sausage, Peppers, and Onions (page 191)

Meringues (page 211) and Tiramisù (page 213)

TRAILBLAZER

I first made this dish on the *Live with Regis and,* at that time, *Kathie Lee* show. This is before the advent of TV chefs. There was no cooking channel. How about that—I was a trailblazer. I had done the show many times, and I suggested that, for this appearance, I would cook with Regis. It was a good segment and we had some fun, although Regis is not much help in the kitchen. He is the greatest but not in the kitchen. We did make a great dish, and in the time allotted, which on TV is not much. It certainly was better than sitting there talking about myself. The funny thing was, after the show, I wanted to make the dish for dinner that night. I went to two markets in the neighborhood, and they were both out of arugula. I guess people liked the recipe.

Pasta with Fresh Tomatoes, Arugula, and Clams

¼ cup extra virgin olive oil
6 garlic cloves, chopped
3 tomatoes, chopped
¼ teaspoon red pepper
1 bunch arugula, rinsed, patted
    dry, and stems removed

2 cans (10 ounces each) baby
    clams
1 pound pasta
Salt and pepper

Heat the oil in a large skillet over medium heat. Add the garlic and sauté until golden brown. Add the tomatoes and red pepper and stir together. Add the arugula and then the clams and simmer for 5 minutes.

Meanwhile cook the pasta in a large pot of boiling salted water until al dente. Take 1½ cups of the starch water from the pasta and add it to the sauce. Simmer the sauce for 5 minutes more. Season with salt and pepper to taste. Drain the pasta, toss with the sauce, and serve.

Serves 4 to 6

"ROKALIROB"

Uncle Phil turned us on to broccoli rabe. It is also called rapini. He calls it "rokalirob." Every Saturday night he cooks for Aunt Frances. He always makes steaks, which he gets from "his guy," and prepares the rokalirob. He always has a gin on the rocks while he works. He says that makes for a happy cook. We don't argue with Uncle Phil. Broccoli rabe is a great side dish for almost anything, but it is also so good with pasta. We also like it with pasta and sausage. With or without the sausage it is a great way to change up a pasta dish.

Pasta with Broccoli Rabe and Sausage

5 hot or sweet Italian sausages

8 tablespoons extra virgin
   olive oil

1 pound pasta, any type you like

1 pound broccoli rabe

5 garlic cloves

½ teaspoon salt

½ teaspoon black pepper

¼ teaspoon red pepper

Grated Parmesan cheese

To cook the sausages, you can use a broiler, a grill, or a skillet. Puncture the sausages all over with a fork. Heat 2 tablespoons of the oil in a large skillet over high heat. Add the sausages and brown on all sides, lowering the heat to medium and cooking about 15 minutes. Discard the oil and fat in the skillet but don't wash the pan.

As always, start the pasta. Bring a large pot of water to a boil, salt it, and bring it back to a boil. Stir in the pasta and cook until al dente. We like to use penne for this, but, again, any kind of macaroni or spaghetti will be fine.

To prepare the broccoli rabe, discard any wilted leaves and trim the ends of the stems. Using a paring knife, peel off the

In the backyard in Malverne, my father's side got together, too.

outer coat of the stems by starting at the bottom and peeling up toward the flower. Some people discard the stems and just cook the flowers and leaves, but if you take the time to peel the stems, it will make them very tender and sweet. Wash the broccoli rabe in cold water and pat dry.

Heat the remaining 6 tablespoons olive oil in the skillet. With the flat side of a chef's knife, crush the garlic, then peel and chop it. Cook the garlic in the oil over medium-high heat until golden. Add the broccoli rabe, salt, and black and red

See that? We're
still smiling!

pepper and sauté for 3 minutes. Pour in 1 cup of the starch water from the pasta and bring to a boil. Cover and continue to boil, stirring occasionally, for about 3 minutes. Reduce the heat to medium-low and simmer for another 5 minutes.

Slice the sausages and add to the broccoli rabe. Cover the pan and cook for 1 minute more. Drain the pasta and combine with the sausages and broccoli rabe. Taste and correct the seasonings. Top with grated Parmesan.

Serves 4 to 6

THE EVERY-NIGHT
DISCUSSION

This wasn't handed down. This one we just made up. It just came into being one night when we couldn't decide what to make for dinner. We don't know about in your house, but in our house what to make for dinner is an every-night conversation. When we have trouble deciding what to make, we have been known to get creative, and most of the time it turns out well. Of course, there have been times when the results were less than spectacular, but that's for another book. It does make me marvel, even more, that my father came up with something good for us to eat every night. This recipe is one of the ones that turned out well.

Pasta with Calamari and Shrimp

½ pound cleaned calamari, cut
    into rings
½ pound shrimp, shelled and
    deveined
1 cup all-purpose flour
½ cup extra virgin olive oil
6 garlic cloves, coarsely chopped

1 pound pasta
½ cup fresh lemon juice
½ cup dry white wine
¼ teaspoon red pepper
¼ teaspoon black pepper
Salt

Dredge the calamari rings and tentacles and the shrimp with flour, shaking off the excess. Heat the oil in a large skillet over medium-high heat. Add the garlic and sauté until golden brown. Remove the garlic from the oil and set aside. Add the shrimp and calamari to the hot oil and sauté until golden, 5 to 8 minutes. Drain on paper towels.

Meanwhile cook the pasta in a large pot of boiling salted water until al dente.

Return the garlic to the skillet and add the lemon juice and white wine. Stir in the red and black pepper, and let it thicken over medium heat for 2 to 3 minutes. Stir in 1 cup of the starch water from the pasta and simmer another minute.

Remove the pan from the heat and add the calamari and shrimp. Drain the pasta and place it in a serving bowl. Add the shrimp, calamari, and sauce to the pasta and toss. Salt to taste.

Serves 4 to 6

My little group helping out— Tracy, BT, Emmie, and Katie

Marc's grandmother
and my brother, Matty

My mother
on the
monkey bars
in Brooklyn

WHAT MY MOTHER COOKED

My mother hasn't gotten much ink in this book so far, and there's a reason for that—she didn't do much cooking. She knew how to cook and was good at it, but my father did most of the cooking. She also got home from work later than he did, and he wouldn't have wanted to wait that long to eat. Marc's grandmother did cook at least two times a year—Thanksgiving and Christmas. On those two special days she made the most famous dish in our world, The Lasagna.

Now on those holidays we also had a full turkey dinner, but her main focus was *the* Lasagna. There is a pretty simple secret to a great lasagna. We're surprised how many people don't know it. The secret is you have to make the meatballs first. You can't just use chopped meat in a lasagna. You have to use meatballs as your chopped meat, so first you have to make them. When we make lasagna, we make a lot of sauce because lasagna really soaks up sauce, and you don't want it to be dry. We make a large Sunday sauce, and for this purpose we make large meatballs. This was a tip from my mom: Since

Holy Communion on Euclid Avenue in Brooklyn—I was such a saint.

you will be crumbling the meatballs anyway, make them bigger to cut down on some of the work. Leave it to my mother to look for a shortcut.

A little bit about my mother, Marc's grandma. She was four foot eleven and always the life of the party. She was the ambitious one in the family. She was always saying, "We should buy the house next store. We should buy the house next store." That the house "next store" wasn't for sale didn't faze her. It was just her way of aspiring to better things for us and also teaching us to dream. She was a hard worker and had a great work ethic. Once when I was young and she was leaving for work not feeling well, I said, "Mom, why don't you stay home? You're sick." She said she had to be there, people were depending on her. I think it was payroll day and she was the head bookkeeper. She was the one who told me I could be

The family in front of the deli they lived above in the 1930s

someone, and she worked hard to get me in and through college. Like I said, she was the ambitious one.

Marc, luckily, got to spend some real time with her. I am so happy about that. My mom was an inspiration and I miss her so. She's been gone thirteen years now and, while doing this book, my son and I spent a lot of time thinking about her and this great family that we were so lucky to be a part of. That time spent remembering has been the most rewarding part of doing this book. It isn't something we do in life that often— sit down and spend some real time remembering. Maybe we should.

Mother's Lasagna

To make *the* Lasagna, start by making a large Sunday Sauce with Meatballs. Add an extra 1 or even 2 cans of tomatoes and another can of tomato paste to the recipe. The amount of meat is the same. Remember to make the meatballs bigger; it saves time. Salt and pepper to taste. When you make the lasagna, make two pans and freeze one. You can freeze portions or the whole tray. As my mother used to say, "Since you're doing it, you might as well make two."

Sunday Sauce with Meatballs (page 127), made without ribs

2 extra cans plum tomatoes with basil

1 pound ricotta cheese

1 extra can tomato paste

2 pounds lasagna noodles

Salt

2 cups grated Parmesan cheese

2 containers (8 ounces each) mozzarella, packed in water

Preheat the oven to 350 degrees.

In a bowl, crumble and crush the meatballs and mix in 1 cup of the sauce. Drain the canned tomatoes in a colander, break-

ing apart the tomatoes with your hands. Discard the pulp. In another bowl mix the ricotta cheese and 1 cup sauce together with a spoon. In another bowl, mix the remaining sauce with the plum tomatoes and tomato paste.

To cook the lasagna noodles, bring a large pot of water to a boil. Add salt and bring back to a boil. Add the noodles and return to a boil. Stir the noodles to make sure they do not stick. Cook for 7 to 8 minutes. Check to see if they are al dente by taking one noodle out and cutting a piece off the end. The noodles should be firm but not hard or soft. To stop the cooking process, remove the pot from the heat and run cold water over the noodles until they are cool enough to handle.

Coat the bottom of a large baking pan with sauce, then add a layer of noodles. Top with some of the crushed meatballs and ricotta, then spread more sauce over all, smoothing it into a layer. Sprinkle with Parmesan and lay out slices of mozzarella. Continue making layers until you reach the top. (If we have ingredients left, we make a smaller lasagna alongside the main attraction.)

To finish, cover with a layer of noodles, sauce, Parmesan, and mozzarella. (Don't be afraid to use sauce.) Cover with foil and bake in the oven for 20 to 30 minutes. My mother used to stick a fork into the middle of the lasagna and feel the end to see if it was hot. Remove the foil and broil for 2 minutes, until browned and a bit crispy on top. Let stand for 15 minutes and serve.

Serves 4 to 6

MAIN COURSES

Doesn't
Emmie
look like
Nicholas?

YOU'RE EATING TOO MUCH BREAD. EAT BREAD!

My father, Marc's grandfather, had the biggest influence on my cooking. I learned to love it watching him. I like to think that I am Marc's big influence. If I am, it's a direct line back to my father. Which I like.

As we said, my father had a saying for everything. Some of his sayings, though, were not clichés or even well known. Some he came up with himself. Once, in a lesson on human nature, he said, "You have to put a lock on the bike to keep the honest people honest." Incredible and, sadly, so true.

Other times he would be saying something about one thing, but there would be another lesson in there too. One such case was his saying "Savor that veal." For those of you who don't eat veal, please put up with it for the sake of the story. We didn't cook any veal dishes for this book—not because we don't eat veal, it's just that chicken is less controversial. Anyway, you know that my father cooked dinner every night and made up the menu. Every other Wednesday he would go to the butcher and get veal cutlets. Remember the butcher? If they weren't good that day, the butcher would tell him, and we might have them on Thursday. Back then, the cutlets were four dollars a pound. That was "beaucoup money," my father would say, but he loved them and so did we. It was special when he made them. He would prepare the cutlets by dipping them in beaten egg and milk and then coat them with seasoned bread crumbs. Then he would sauté them in olive oil and stack them with paper towels between each layer. He would make a salad, and the salad dressing was great with the veal. A vegetable for the side, maybe canned creamed corn. Ahh, those were the days. A potato of some kind, baked or french fried. He would send me to the store for Italian bread, as he did almost every night. But when we had veal cutlets, he would want two loaves. Most nights you could get reprimanded for eating too much bread. On veal cutlet night, you were supposed to eat too much bread. Hence the chapter title, "You're eating too much bread. Eat bread!" How much bread we were supposed to eat depended on what night it was and what we were having. Then, while we were eating, he would say, "Savor that veal." Of course, he meant slow down and enjoy the dinner, at least chew, but it's come to mean so much more to Marc and me.

All this remembering we did for this book made us think about how fast things come and go, so many wonderful people who are no longer with us. So "savor that veal" has come to mean that we should take notice, be there, experience all there is, wherever we are. Take nothing for granted and, most importantly, appreciate the people around you—your family and your friends. Enjoy and, yes, savor every minute or at least as many as you can. My dad died when Marc was twelve and I was thirty-two. Just when we needed him, he was gone. Savor that veal.

My son has memories of his grandfather, so I'll let him tell you:

Thanks, Dad. I'll never forget the time my grandfather took me fluke fishing. Fluke are big, flat bottom fish that are delicious when filleted. I was probably six or seven years old, and we went on a public charter fishing boat near Jones Beach, on Long Island. I remember he showed me how to tie a fishing knot, and I still use that knot whenever I fish. I remember how strong he was. Another really vivid memory of him is when he was real sick and living with my father and me at the house in Hollywood Hills. He had cancer from smoking cigarettes, and my father had brought him to California so we could take care of him. My father was out working on his show *Taxi,* and I was playing around the house. I went from playing music in my room to dragging all my GI Joe men out to the living room. Then I wanted to play video games, and after five minutes of that, I decided to go swimming. My grandfather, who was sitting back this whole time watching me do all these things, finally snapped, "Will you make up your mind already?!" I said I was sorry. He was real sick, and I know I was driving him nuts that day. Now when I watch my son go from one toy to the next, sometimes it makes me think of my grandfather and how much I really miss him.

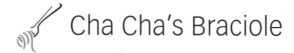

Cha Cha's Braciole

Braciole holds a special place not only for us but also for most Italians. There is always a braciole stand at every Italian street feast. During the famous New York City Feast of San Gennaro, you can get one from my friend at Cha Cha's Braciole Stand on Mulberry Street in Little Italy. It consists of a pounded piece of steak that is stuffed and rolled, then either grilled or browned in garlic and oil and cooked in sauce. We didn't have braciole that often growing up, except when we ate at Aunt Fran and Uncle Phil's. Aunt Fran's sauce always had braciole because Uncle Phil loved it. Braciole is usually a part of a sauce, but sometimes we make it as a main course, alone, or with a sauce of its own. That almost rhymes.

Braciole

1 pound skirt steak, bottom round, or flank steak
½ cup extra virgin olive oil, or as needed
Salt and pepper

2 eggs
1 cup seasoned dried bread crumbs
6 garlic cloves, finely chopped
1 cup grated Parmesan cheese

Sauce

⅓ cup extra virgin olive oil

3 garlic cloves, chopped

1 small to medium onion, chopped

1 can (35 ounces) plum tomatoes with basil

½ cup red wine

¼ teaspoon red pepper

Salt and pepper

½ cup fresh basil leaves, slivered

Braciole is usually made with bottom round or flank steak. We like to use skirt steak. Whatever you use you want the meat to be one or two thin, long pieces, as you will roll the meat up. If you use flank or bottom round, you will have to slice it first and then pound it thin. Skirt steak starts out thinner and is easier to pound. Brush the pounded meat with some of the olive oil, then season with salt and pepper.

Hard-boil the eggs. Peel the eggs and quarter. Mix the bread crumbs and garlic. Add olive oil and wet thoroughly. Spread the mixture over the meat and sprinkle with Parmesan.

Place the eggs at the end of the meat, roll up compactly, and secure with toothpicks. (If you are making these for Sunday Sauce [page 127], brown them as you do the meatballs and ribs.)

Heat the olive oil in a large saucepan over medium-high heat. Add the garlic and onion and sauté for about 4 minutes, until the onion is wilted. Add the braciole and brown on all sides. With your hands, crush the tomatoes in a bowl, removing the tops and cores. Add the remaining juice from the can. Add the tomatoes, wine, red pepper, and salt and pepper to taste to the pot. Bring to a boil, stirring occasionally. Reduce the heat and simmer, uncovered, for 1 hour. Add the basil and simmer for another 10 minutes. Check the seasonings. Serve with pasta or just remove the toothpicks, slice the braciole, and serve in the sauce.

Serves 4 to 6

THE MOUSSE IS LOOSE

Emmie has always been a bit of a rebel and a picky eater. Once when she was five, the four of us went out to dinner. We sat down, and when the waitress came over, my daughter Katie ordered a chicken dish, Tracy, my wife, ordered a steak, and Emmie, some pasta. I asked the waitress what the special was, and she said it was roast duck. I said, "Great, I'll have the duck." Emmie turned to me and said, "Duck? A quack, quack duck? You can't eat a duck!" I said, "Sweetheart, that's what we do. I mean it's food. Katie's having chicken. Mom is having steak. Where do you think that comes from?" She gave me a look that said we couldn't be related and that was the end of it until dessert. The waitress said the special dessert that night was chocolate mousse. Without missing a beat, Emmie said, "Oh no, not another animal!"

Chicken Parm

This dish is my daughter Emmie's favorite. We used to make it with veal, but she didn't like that so we went to chicken. Many people have trouble eating veal for one reason or another. We totally understand. For my father it was the cost, "beaucoup money." You can substitute veal cutlets, and we have even tried shrimp and pork. Pork was really good and it's an alliteration—pork parmigiana.

6 chicken cutlets

2 eggs, beaten

3 tablespoons milk

1 cup seasoned dried bread
   crumbs

1 cup extra virgin olive oil

Quick or Date Sauce
   (page 113)

1 package (8 ounces)
   mozzarella, packed in water
   and thinly sliced

1 cup grated Parmesan cheese

Preheat the oven to 375 degrees.

Pound the cutlets thin. Beat the eggs with the milk in a shallow bowl. Put the bread crumbs in a second bowl. Coat the cutlets, one at a time, first with the egg, then with the bread crumbs. Heat the olive oil in a large skillet over medium-high heat until hot. Add as many cutlets as will fit in a single layer and sauté until golden brown, about 2 minutes a side. Drain on paper towels. Repeat with any remaining cutlets.

Coat the bottom of a large baking pan with sauce and line the pan with the cutlets. Cover with sauce and spread the slices of mozzarella and the Parmesan on top. Cover with foil and bake for 10 to 15 minutes. Remove the foil and broil for 2 minutes, until the top is a bit brown and crispy.

Serves 4 to 6

Eggplant Parm

Everyone in our family loves this dish. I have loved it since I was a kid. I would come home from elementary school, in Brooklyn, and there on the top of the stove would be a dinner plate covered with a circle of eggplant parmigiana. That was the way Great-grandma made it. When I say Great-grandma, I do mean my mother's mother, my grandmother, Marc's great-grandmother. By the way, she was great. About four foot nine with blue eyes and the happiest laugh you've ever heard. She would layer the eggplant in a circle on a dinner plate. You would cut it like a pie and have a piece. When you took a forkful, the cheese and the sauce would almost sting your mouth. She didn't use ricotta, just Parmesan. We make it the same way she did.

2 large eggplants
Salt
2 eggs, beaten
3 tablespoons milk
2 cups seasoned dried bread crumbs
1 cup extra virgin olive oil

Quick or Date Sauce (page 113)
1 cup grated Parmesan cheese
1 package (8 ounces) mozzarella, packed in water and thinly sliced
1 cup ricotta cheese (optional)

Preheat the oven to 375 degrees.

Cut the ends off the eggplant and peel it with a vegetable peeler or a knife. (We think the skin is bitter.) Cut the eggplant into thin slices. (We like them thin, but it's fine if they are thicker.) Put the slices in a colander. Sprinkle with salt and place a plate on top. Let drain for 1 hour. We have skipped this step from time to time if we didn't have the hour. The world did not come to an end.

Beat the eggs with the milk in a shallow bowl. Put the bread crumbs in a second bowl. Coat the eggplant slices, one at a time, with the eggs, then with the bread crumbs. Heat the olive oil in a large skillet over high heat until hot. The eggplant should sizzle when you put it in the oil. Cook the slices, turning once, until golden brown. Drain on paper towels.

Cover the bottom of a large baking pan with tomato sauce and place a layer of eggplant on top. Sprinkle the Parmesan over the eggplant, then add a layer of sliced mozzarella. (If using ricotta cheese, just spoon some into each layer.) Continue making layers and finish the top with sauce and cheese.

Cover with foil and bake in the oven for 10 to 15 minutes. Uncover and broil for 2 minutes, until the top is a bit brown and crispy. Let stand for a few minutes, then serve right from the baking pan.

Serves 4 to 6

Chicken with Lemon and Garlic

Growing up, this was one of my very favorite dishes. It's a great way to do something different with chicken and it's fairly easy. We had always prepared it the way my father did until a few years ago when we used the broiler instead. We thought we would give you both ways and let you be the decider. That really isn't a shot at President Bush—it just made us laugh. Well, maybe it is a shot.

Dad's Way

1 cup fresh lemon juice
1 cup extra virgin olive oil
8 garlic cloves, chopped

1 chicken (about 3 pounds), cut
    into 8 pieces
2 large baking potatoes
Salt and pepper

Broiler Way

All of the above
½ teaspoon dried oregano

2 tablespoons balsamic vinegar

Preheat the oven to 375 degrees.

My father's way: Whisk the lemon juice, olive oil, and garlic together. Put the chicken pieces in a large baking pan. Peel the potatoes, cut into 2-inch pieces, and toss with the lemon mixture. Spread the potatoes around the chicken. Season with salt and pepper. Pour the remaining lemon mixture over the chicken and potatoes and turn to coat evenly. At this point my father would say he wished he had some time to let it marinate in the refrigerator. He never did and it was always great. If you have time, an hour would be good.

Bake, turning the chicken and potatoes occasionally to brown all sides, until the juices run clear when the thigh is pricked, about 1 hour.

The broiler way: Add the oregano and balsamic vinegar to the marinade. Mix it in a large bowl and set aside. Cut the potatoes into 2-inch pieces and arrange on a sided cookie sheet or shallow roasting pan with the chicken. Under a hot broiler, cook the chicken and potatoes, turning once, until golden brown, about 30 minutes. Toss the chicken in the marinade to coat, and place it back under the broiler for 3 minutes. Turn the chicken over, pour the rest of the marinade over it, and broil for another 2 minutes. Pour the juices and marinade from the pan into a saucepan and cook over high heat for 1 minute. Arrange the chicken on a platter, cover with the sauce, and serve.

Serves 4

White Fish and Shrimp with Potatoes and Onions in a Lemon, Wine, and Butter Sauce

Talk about a long title. We have been cooking and eating this for the last three nights, trying to get it right. You can make this recipe with just the fish. Any white-fleshed fish is good: orange roughy, sole, flounder, etc. We have been using roughy because it looked the best at the market. Don't be afraid to ask the counter person what's good. They love to tell you and then have you come back happy the next time. It helps to build a relationship with the people who sell you food. Reach out and ask for help and you will be rewarded with some inside info.

1 medium potato
1 medium onion
1 cup fresh lemon juice
1 cup dry white wine
2 tablespoons butter
¼ teaspoon salt

¼ teaspoon red pepper
½ teaspoon black pepper
2 white-fleshed fish fillets
  (about 1 pound)
6 large shrimp, shelled and
  deveined

Preheat the oven to 375 degrees.

Peel the potato and boil in water to cover for 3 minutes, then simmer for 2 minutes more. Drain and transfer the potato to a bowl of cold water. Thinly slice the onion.

Mix the lemon juice, wine, butter, salt, and red and black pepper in a medium-size baking pan. Place in the oven to melt the butter. Remove the pan and stir, mixing all ingredients thoroughly. Place the fish in the pan and turn to coat evenly. Cut the potato into thin slices, spread the potatoes and onion around and over the fish, and turn to coat all.

Cover the pan with foil and bake for 15 minutes. Remove the foil. Add the shrimp and broil for 2 minutes, until it gets a bit brown on top. Serve right out of the pan.

Serves 4 to 6

 # Broiled White Fish

This dish is a simple, healthful, and delicious way to get fish into your diet. Any white-fleshed fish, such as orange roughy, sole, or flounder, will work.

2 white-fleshed fish fillets
  (about 1 pound)
2 tablespoons extra virgin
  olive oil
1 tablespoon all-purpose flour

1 tablespoon seasoned dried
  bread crumbs
1 tablespoon butter
Salt and pepper
½ cup dry white wine
½ cup fresh lemon juice

Preheat the broiler. You want it hot.

Brush the fish fillets with the olive oil and place them in a roasting or baking pan. Sprinkle the flour and bread crumbs over the fish and dot with butter. Season with salt and pepper. Pour the wine and lemon juice into the pan. Broil for 5 to 6 minutes, or until the flesh of the fish flakes when touched with a fork. You should have a nice golden color to the fish as well. We told you it was easy.

Serves 4

 # Shrimp Scampi

Everybody loves scampi. It is a favorite of my girls, and when they're happy, I'm happy. It's easy to make but you have to know the ingredients. There are some surprises.

16 large shrimp (about 1 pound), shelled and deveined
½ cup all-purpose flour
⅓ cup extra virgin olive oil
2 tablespoons butter
6 garlic cloves, chopped
1 cup dry white wine
1 cup fresh lemon juice
1 tablespoon Worcestershire sauce
½ cup chicken broth
Salt and pepper
1 tablespoon chopped fresh parsley
¼ teaspoon paprika

Dredge the shrimp with the flour, shaking off the excess. Heat the oil and butter in a large skillet until hot. Add the garlic and sauté until golden. Add the shrimp and sauté for about 3 minutes a side. Remove the shrimp from the pan.

Add the wine, lemon juice, Worcestershire sauce, chicken broth, and salt and pepper to taste to the pan. Bring to a boil, then reduce the heat and simmer for 2 minutes. Return the shrimp to the pan, add the parsley and paprika, and simmer for 2 minutes more. Serve with a great loaf of Italian bread.

Serves 4

Even on a movie set we eat and drink.

Roasted Chicken and Potatoes

We love to roast chicken. We love the way the house smells as the chicken cooks. Add a vegetable and a salad and you have a very nice dinner. Corn on the cob or artichokes are great.

1 chicken (about 3 pounds)
1 lemon, halved
2 tablespoons butter, at room temperature
Salt and pepper

2 large potatoes, peeled and cut into bite-sized pieces
3 tablespoons extra virgin olive oil

Preheat the oven to 450 degrees.

Rinse the chicken well and pat dry. Squeeze the lemon into the cavity and all over the skin. Put the squeezed lemon halves in the cavity. Rub the butter all over the chicken. Place the chicken on a rack in a roasting pan and season with salt and pepper to taste.

Toss the potatoes with the olive oil and salt and pepper and spread around the chicken. Roast for about 1 hour. The chicken is done when juices run clear when you prick the thigh of the bird. The potatoes should be brown and crispy. Place the pan under the broiler to crisp it up. Let the chicken sit for a few minutes before carving.

Serves 4 to 6

The backyard grill

 # Ribs

We cook spareribs in our Sunday sauce. The family recipe actually called for pork neck bones, which were in the sauce just to add flavor. Marc and I figured spareribs would be better because you would still get the flavor and you could eat them. After they have cooked in the sauce, the meat falls off the bone. Another way to make ribs is to roast them in the oven. (This works for both pork and beef ribs.) In the summer we like to grill them outside. We make a marinade and brush the ribs with it as we grill them. For oven roasting we cut the rack into individual ribs.

1 rack pork spareribs or beef
   shortribs, cut into individual
   ribs
Salt and pepper
½ cup extra virgin olive oil
8 garlic cloves, chopped

1 can (14 ounces) chicken broth
1 cup dry white wine
½ cup red wine vinegar
½ cup honey
1 teaspoon red pepper

Preheat the oven to 400 degrees.

Season the ribs with salt and pepper and put them in a large baking pan. Mix the olive oil and garlic, pour over the ribs, and toss to coat evenly. Pour the chicken broth over all and roast for 1 hour, turning the ribs frequently.

Whisk the wine, vinegar, honey, and red pepper together in a mixing bowl. Brush the ribs with the mixture and pour the rest over the top. Roast for another 15 to 20 minutes, turning the ribs frequently. Serve with Danza Everyday Salad (page 53).

Serves 4 to 6

Sausage, Peppers, and Onions

It's funny that each time Marc and I start to write a recipe, we say, "This is our favorite. We love this one." I guess that means that we love all this food, and we really love sausage, peppers, and onions. We are pretty certain all Italians love sausage and peppers. In our family, we actually have a gentleman who had a sausage and peppers truck. His name is Uncle Stucky, and his truck was Stucky's Sausage and Peppers. He's one of those people you call uncle, but he wasn't really

That's my Emmie.

12 hot or sweet Italian sausages
½ cup extra virgin olive oil
4 green bell peppers, cored,
  seeded, and cut into strips

1 large onion, sliced
Salt and pepper

---

related. He certainly acted as a cool uncle when we stopped at the truck for a sandwich. Stucky was really Uncle Phil's cousin. We know it's confusing, but the dish isn't.

Preheat the oven to 400 degrees.

Prick the sausages all over with a fork. Heat 3 tablespoons of the olive oil in a large skillet over high heat, Add the sausages and brown on all sides, about 8 minutes, reducing the heat to medium-high as the sausages cook. Put the peppers and

See how happy sausage and peppers make us?

onion in a large baking pan. Drizzle with the remaining oil, sprinkle with salt and pepper to taste, and toss well. Add the sausages to the pan and cover with foil. Bake for 20 minutes. Remove the foil, stir, and cook for another 5 minutes. The peppers should be tender but not mushy.

Serves 4 to 6

 # Frying Steaks

When we had steaks for dinner, my father made them in a frying pan on the stove. You don't see that much anymore. Nowadays, they're grilled or broiled but rarely fried. This recipe uses my father's method of cooking steaks and adds peppers, white mushrooms, tomatoes, garlic, and fresh basil. It is a great way to do something different with steak, other than just grilling.

4 tablespoons extra virgin
   olive oil
3 garlic cloves, chopped
1 medium onion, chopped
1 cup white mushrooms, sliced
2 bell peppers, cored, seeded,
   and cut into strips
Salt and pepper

1 can (35 ounces) plum
   tomatoes with basil
½ teaspoon red pepper
½ cup fresh basil leaves, cut into
   slivers
2 beef rib-eye steaks
   (1 to 1½ pounds)

Heat 3 tablespoons of the olive oil in a large skillet over medium-high heat. Add the garlic and sauté until lightly browned. Add the onion, mushrooms, peppers, and salt and pepper to taste and cook until wilted, about 5 minutes.

With your hands, remove the tops and cores from the tomatoes and squeeze the rest into a bowl. Add the tomatoes with the remaining juice in the can to the pan. Stir in the red pepper and bring to a boil. Reduce the heat and simmer for 10 minutes. Add the basil and simmer for another 5 minutes.

Brush the steaks with the remaining tablespoon olive oil and fry them in a skillet over high heat for 4 to 5 minutes a side. Slice the steaks against the grain, add to the sauce, and simmer for 1 minute. Serve on a platter.

Serves 4 to 6

Marc's Tangerine-Honey Chicken with Chipotle Glaze

Here is another one of my son's recipes. Speak, son:

With a tangerine tree in my backyard, I thought it would be cool to cook with my own tangerines. This recipe uses a lot of tangerines, so if you don't have a tree, be sure to get plenty from the store, more than a dozen. This dish was inspired by my love for citrus and chicken—they go together so well. In the summer I like to stay out of the kitchen and to grill as much as possible. So many flavors come out of this dish—it's an excellent way to spend an evening by the barby.

Glaze

2 cups fresh tangerine juice
5 tablespoons honey
¼ cup soy sauce

2 tablespoons finely grated
   tangerine or orange zest
2 teaspoons minced canned
   chipotle chile in adobo sauce★

★Chipotle chiles—dried, smoked jalapeños canned in adobo, a spicy tomato sauce—are available at supermarkets, specialty stores, and Latin markets.

Chicken

2 tablespoons finely grated
  tangerine or orange zest
1 cup fresh tangerine or orange
  juice
⅓ cup chopped fresh parsley
⅓ cup chopped fresh cilantro
3 tablespoons chopped fresh thyme
3 tablespoons minced fresh
  ginger

3 tablespoons unseasoned rice
  vinegar
2 tablespoons extra virgin
  olive oil
1 teaspoon coarse salt, plus more
  as needed
1 chicken (2¾ to 3 pounds),
  quartered, backbone removed

For the glaze, boil the juice, honey, and soy sauce in a heavy medium saucepan until reduced to ⅔ cup, about 20 minutes. Mix in the citrus zest and chipotle.

For the chicken, whisk the citrus zest and juice, the parsley, cilantro, thyme, ginger, vinegar, oil, and salt in a 13 x 9-inch glass baking dish to blend. Add the chicken and turn to coat with the marinade. Cover and refrigerate for at least 2 hours and up to 1 day, turning the pieces occasionally.

Spray a grill rack with vegetable oil cooking spray and prepare the barbecue (medium-low heat). Remove the chicken from the marinade; discard the marinade. Sprinkle the chicken lightly with salt. Grill the chicken until cooked through, turning and repositioning it occasionally for even cooking, about 20 minutes. Brush the chicken all over with the glaze and grill for 2 minutes more on each side. Transfer the chicken to a platter. Serve, passing the remaining glaze separately.

Serves 4

 # Taiedda

To tell the truth, I had never heard of this dish. But my son, Marc, loves it and says, "This is an Italian dish. Like many foods that come from Southern Italy, it has peasant origins."

½ cup extra virgin olive oil
2 garlic cloves, chopped
1½ pounds potatoes, peeled and
   thinly sliced
1 onion, thinly sliced
Handful of fresh Chinese pea
   pods

2 halibut fillets
   (about 1 to 1½ pounds)
Salt and pepper
3 tablespoons melted butter
½ cup dry white wine
3 tablespoons seasoned dried
   bread crumbs
Chopped fresh basil leaves

Preheat the oven to 375 degrees.

Butter the bottom and sides of a 10 x 8-inch baking dish.

Heat the oil in a large skillet. Add the garlic and sauté until it begins to soften. Add a layer of potatoes and cook over medium-high heat just until golden. Flip the potatoes and

I love my son.

cook the other side until golden. Drain on paper towels and repeat with any remaining potatoes.

Place half the potatoes in the buttered dish, then half the onion, a few of the peas, and half of the fish. Sprinkle with salt and pepper to taste and then drizzle with half the butter.

Make a second layer with the remaining potatoes, onion, peas, fish, and salt and pepper to taste. Pour the wine over the top. Let it seep down through the fish, then sprinkle the bread crumbs on top. Drizzle with the remaining butter. Cover with foil and bake for 20 to 30 minutes. Remove the foil and brown the bread crumbs under the broiler for 2 to 3 minutes. Sprinkle the basil over all before serving.

Serves 4 to 6

Notice the Band-Aid.

Aunt Rose's Fusilli Casserole

Aunt Rose was an institution. A wonderful, solid source of strength, smart and wise, my mother's older sister was another surrogate parent to me and my son. We love thinking about her, so here's one of her favorites.

This dish is much like *the* Lasagna and uses meatballs in the same way. We have made a variation using a quick sauce and sliced sausages, but usually it's Sunday Sauce with Meatballs. In this recipe we use hard-boiled eggs, which surprisingly go great with tomato sauce.

4 eggs
1 large eggplant
½ cup extra virgin olive oil
Salt
2 pounds fusilli

Sunday Sauce with Meatballs (page 127), made without the ribs
2 cups grated Parmesan cheese

Preheat the oven to 375 degrees.

Aunt Rose
and Uncle Vinny

Here's how Aunt Rose made it: Hard-boil the eggs, remove from the water, and cool. Peel and quarter. Peel the eggplant and cut into 1-inch pieces. Heat the olive oil in a large skillet over medium-high heat. Add the eggplant and sauté until lightly browned. Drain on paper towels.

Meanwhile bring a large pot of water to a boil for the fusilli. Add 2 tablespoons salt and bring the water back to a boil. Stir in the fusilli and cook until al dente, about 7 minutes. Remove the pot from the heat and put it in the sink. Run cold water into the pot to cool the water and stop the cooking process. The pasta should be cool enough to handle.

Take the finished meatballs and crumble 6 of them in a mixing bowl. Add 1 cup of the sauce and mix. Drain the pasta. Make a layer of pasta in the bottom of a 10 x 8-inch baking pan. Spread some of the meatball mixture, pieces of eggplant, and some of the quartered eggs over the fusilli. Cover with sauce and sprinkle with Parmesan. Make layers with the remaining fusilli and all the other ingredients to the top of the pan, finishing with a layer of the fusilli, sauce, and cheese.

Cover the pan with foil and bake for 15 to 20 minutes. Remove the foil and broil for about 2 minutes, until the top is a bit browned and crispy.

Serves 4 to 6

DESSERTS

Grandma's
backyard
birthday

NOT BIG BAKERS

We are not big bakers. When we have a dinner, somebody else usually brings a cake or some pastry. But you can't have a cookbook without desserts, so Marc and I started a dessert discussion, trying to figure out which desserts we wanted to make. The conversation, inevitably, turned to dessert at our family dinners. We remembered that by the time we got to dessert, it was a glorious cacophony of love, laughter, and satisfaction. By then, some of the uncles would have their belts open and all of them would have had a few drinks. Uncle Phil drinks gin, my father and uncles Mike, John, and Vinny drink Scotch. They all, including the aunts, would have had wine, so it was loud. Then the desserts would come out. Pastry, cookies, sometimes Grandma's fig cookies, and when dinner was at Aunt Rose's, a ricotta cheesecake, which we absolutely loved. Now the cousins have had sugar and the scene reaches a crescendo. Cousins Jimmy and Charles are running around. Cousin Anthony is picking those little nuts off the cookies and throwing them at me. My brother, Matty, is eating the cookies without the nuts. The celebration would go on and on.

Leaving was tough, but baking really isn't, at least not these recipes. We decided on three. They all make you look like you really know what you're doing, although they are all rather simple. One comes from Aunt Rose, one comes from an actor I worked with (it's his mother's recipe for meringues), and Marc and I made a tiramisù.

Ricotta Cheesecake

Some desserts look as good as they taste. This is one of them. It is a big favorite of ours, not too sweet, just right.

1 pound ricotta cheese
½ cup golden raisins
¼ cup rum
Softened butter for greasing
   the pan
⅓ cup dried bread crumbs
1 cup plus 2 tablespoons sugar

5 large eggs, separated
¼ teaspoon salt
Grated zest of 1 orange and
   1 lemon
½ cup heavy cream
½ cup pine nuts

Line a colander with a coffee filter and set the colander inside a larger bowl. Put the ricotta in the colander, cover with plastic wrap, and let drain in the refrigerator for several hours or overnight. Discard any liquid.

Soak the raisins in the rum for 15 minutes.

Preheat the oven to 325 degrees. Coat the sides and bottom of a 9-inch springform cake pan with softened butter. Mix the bread crumbs and 2 tablespoons sugar. Pour the bread crumb mixture into the buttered pan and coat generously, tapping the sides of the pan as you turn it. Reserve the excess.

Whisk the egg yolks, 1 cup sugar, and the salt together in a large bowl. Add the drained ricotta and lemon and orange zest and mix thoroughly by hand. Stir in the cream, pine nuts, and raisins with rum.

Beat the egg whites with a mixer until they form stiff, firm peaks when you lift out the beater. Using a spatula, fold the egg whites into the ricotta mixture. Pour the mixture into the pan and gently sprinkle the excess bread crumbs over the top.

Bake 1¼ hours. Let cool completely before serving.

Serves 6 to 8

 # Meringues

This recipe was given to me by an actor I worked with on Broadway. We were doing Arthur Miller's *A View from the Bridge.* His name is David Gray. He played Rodolfo, and I played Eddie Carbone. It is a wonderful and very serious play—and for Italians it is *Streetcar.* It was both of our Broadway debuts and we became good friends. One day in his dressing room, I noticed these cookies he had on his table. I had one and asked where they came from. He told me his mother had been making them for as long as he could remember.

Later he told his mom how much I liked them, so she made some for me and gave me the recipe. Being on Broadway is great, and you get recipes too.

We now make them sometimes for Sunday dinner. The kids really like them, and they are great with a cup of strong coffee.

3 large egg whites, at room
    temperature
1 teaspoon vanilla extract
¼ teaspoon cream of tartar

1 cup sugar
Dark chocolate mini chips
    (optional)

Preheat the oven to 300 degrees.

Start with room-temperature egg whites. If the eggs have been refrigerated, separate them and let the whites stand in a mixing bowl for about 1 hour. Add the vanilla and the cream of tartar to the egg whites and beat with an electric mixer until soft peaks form. Beat in the sugar gradually until completely mixed. The cookies can be made plain or you can fold in the mini chips.

Line a cookie sheet with wax paper, and using a tablespoon, spoon the batter onto the wax paper. Bake the meringues for 40 minutes. Turn the oven off and leave the cookies in the oven for 1 hour. Remove the cookies from the oven, peel off the wax paper, and serve.

Makes about 2 dozen cookies

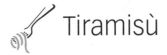 # Tiramisù

This is the classic Italian dessert. We have always loved it, and where we grew up, there was always a bakery that made a great one. It is an intimidating-looking dessert but really fairly simple to make. You will need a double boiler. We didn't have one, so we rigged a pot in a pot.

4 large eggs, separated
1 pint heavy cream
1 cup sugar
½ pound mascarpone cheese
¼ cup Cognac

24 ladyfingers, store-bought
2 cups brewed espresso coffee,
    cooled
1 tablespoon unsweetened cocoa
    powder

Using an electric mixer, beat the egg whites until firm peaks form. Bring water to a boil in the bottom of a double boiler. In the top, beat the egg yolks until thick. In another bowl beat the cream until firm peaks form.

Beat the sugar, mascarpone, and Cognac in a mixing bowl until smooth. Fold in the egg whites, thickened yolks, and whipped cream until thoroughly blended.

Dip each ladyfinger in the espresso and arrange over the bottom and up the sides of a 2- to 3-quart glass or serving bowl. Spread with half the egg mixture. Top with the remaining ladyfingers, each one soaked in espresso, and cover with the remaining egg mixture. Sprinkle the cocoa over the top and refrigerate for at least 1 hour.

P.S. Some folks fear raw eggs. Our family has never been among them. But if you worry, make a different dessert. They're all good.

Serves 8 to 10

FINAL WORDS

We handed in the book and were happy to hear that our editor, Beth, and our publisher, Susan, liked what we had written. There was a *but,* though. They wanted more—more stories and more recipes. We resisted at first saying, "Hey, what are we writing here, the *Joy of Cooking*?" Beth simmered us down with how much she liked what we had written so far (she's good), but then she said if we wanted a real book, we would have to come up with more.

So, being the professionals we are, we went back to work. Marc said he would write the lobster story, and I thought I would write about the time I ran away from home when I was ten and chose the wrong aunt's house to go to.

It all started as a regular day at Blessed Sacrament School in Brooklyn. The school building was on one side of Euclid Avenue, and the cathedral-sized church, across the street, on the other. Next to the church was the schoolyard and the playground. The school building was impressive, especially for the neighborhood. Somehow it looked as strict as it actually was.

There was an entrance for the boys and one for the girls.

Above each entrance, in the stonework, it said either "Boys" or "Girls." You had to use your entrance. The reason I tell you all this is to give you a sense of the environment in which this incident took place. I was in the fifth grade. I was "accelerated." I was a pretty good student but did get into my small troubles. It was so strict that it was pretty easy to break one of the rules eventually.

That year I had a teacher who was not a nun. Her name was Miss Shay. She was probably in her forties and had been teaching at the school a long time. She was legendary for being tough. Remember, this was a time when there was still corporal punishment in the schools, and the nuns would really give it to you. The lay teachers, I think that's what they were called, meaning not nuns or priests, would sometimes try to out-discipline the nuns. Miss Shay was one of those.

I was sitting towards the back of the classroom when I noticed two of my friends laughing and whispering to each other. Then one of them, a kid named Joey Graham, a good friend of mine, passed a piece of paper to the kid in front of him. That kid passed it on until it got to the girl it was intended for in the front row. Her name was Geraldine, and she had the worst continuing case of chapped lips you could ever imagine. Not just chapped though. Because she was constantly licking her skin with her tongue, from her nose to her chin, her lips were cracked and on some days even bloody. I had no idea, when she immediately raised her hand and reported to Miss Shay that someone had written her a love note, that I would soon be in a lot of trouble. By the way, back then it was Miss, not Ms., which might explain why Miss Shay was so hard to get along with. Miss Shay came down the aisle and took the note. I couldn't wait to see who had broken the no-notes-in-class rule. She read the note out loud. It went something like this: "Dear Geraldine, I have loved you ever since school began and I would love to kiss you on your lips." There was a loud groan in the classroom as everyone waited for the sender to be named. Miss Shay took off her glasses, letting them hang from the cord around her neck, and looked in my direction. She didn't say a word, as if for dramatic effect. Then she said, holding the note in front of her, "Signed, Anthony Iadanza." At first I was so shocked to hear my name that I thought I had imagined it. But when she came to my seat and got me, I figured it was real. I started to protest but then decided to just take the punishment and save my friends. She wouldn't have believed me anyway, as this was not my first offense, although I had never written a note to the chapped-lipped girl before.

Each classroom had a closet in the front of the room. Those closets were where the teachers took you when you did something wrong, although sometimes they would just whack you in front of the class. She took me in the closet and slapped me a couple of times. It really wasn't that bad. On the way out she told me I would have to write "I must not write notes in class" six hundred times.

When school broke for lunch, I was waiting for my two friends by the schoolyard. They were laughing, and I wasn't that upset myself, but I pushed Joey and he fell. When the back of his arm hit the curb and made the loudest crack I had ever heard, I had a feeling my troubles were just beginning. His arm was broken and he was crying and I had done it. Yes, it was an accident but this, I thought, would be too much to explain to Miss Shay. Or to my parents. I said I was sorry to Joey and took off before the nuns got there.

I lived a block away up Euclid Avenue and would sometimes go home for lunch. So that's where I went. I made myself a sandwich and thought about my situation. I knew I was in trouble and worried about the consequences, which could be dire, considering my father. But the thing that really bothered me was that I never wanted to disappoint my parents and certainly, this chain of events would do just that. What can I tell you? I was ten. So I wrote my mother and father a goodbye letter. I told them how sorry I was and how they would be much better off without me. (Martyr?) I told them how much I loved them and signed the letter, "Goodbye, your son, Anthony." It was a great letter. The only problem was I folded it up way too small and then put it under the obligatory ashtray on the kitchen table. Dick Tracy would have had trouble finding it.

Anyway, it was now about twelve thirty and it was a beautiful day. I walked out of the house and out of the neighborhood. I had decided that I would run away to my Uncle Vinny's in Patchogue on Long Island. That was about sixty miles away, but it didn't matter because my uncle would understand. I knew my way there because whenever our family would drive to one of the Long Island relatives', we

My father and
Uncle Vinny

would play a game to see who could remember the route. I was always a good memorizer. So I walked to Conduit Boulevard, which is what Atlantic Avenue turns into, then east until the Conduit ran into the Belt Parkway. My father would always get on the highway there, and so I did too.

There I was in my Catholic school uniform, walking along the side of the Belt Parkway. As the cars whizzed by I made sure I had some protection. I found an old rusty tire iron. Nobody was going to mess with this Brooklyn boy. I kept walking and finally reached where the Belt Parkway meets Sunrise Highway. I had been walking now for about five hours and was tired and really hungry. Just before Sunrise Highway, on the service road, I saw a hot dog stand. The man was packing up like he was finished for the day. I walked over wanting to ask how much farther I had to go. I was also

Uncle Phil—so cool

hoping he might give me a hot dog because I had no money.
I guess I didn't think of everything.

By this time I had decided I would never make it to
Patchogue and would instead go to my uncle Phil's in Lynbrook. He probably wouldn't understand as well as Uncle
Vinny, but he was closer. My aunt Fran was sweet and my
cousins Anthony, Jimmy, and Geri would be fun. I asked the
hot dog man how much farther it was to Lynbrook. He
pointed east and said, as he looked around, "It's a ways.
Where's your car?" I looked at him with hungry eyes and said
it was around the corner. I don't think he believed me. He
shrugged and pushed off, his cart making a clanging sound as
he left.

Still hungry, I got back on the road. I stayed left on the Belt until it turned into the Southern State Parkway. The side of the highway in Long Island was nicer than in Brooklyn. It was almost like a park. I kept walking, without incident, until I got to exit fifteen, Franklin Avenue. I got off the highway and walked down Franklin Avenue to my aunt and uncle's street. It was about three miles. I think the whole trip was about twenty-five miles.

It was just dinner time when I got to their house, and I could hear my cousins, in the dining room, sitting down to eat. I was pretty happy. I was actually able to find their house and just in time for dinner. Just as I was about to knock on the door, my uncle, whose booming voice we have spoken of earlier in the book, started to, shall we say, raise that voice at one of my cousins. Outside, I thought, maybe this is the wrong aunt and uncle. Can you imagine how scary he must have sounded? I was so hungry. Then I thought, what about Aunt Sadie and Uncle Mike? They lived just around the corner. We told you the family liked to live close to each other. So I walked down the block, made the right turn, crossed the street, and saw my aunt Sadie sweeping the sidewalk. She was always neat. She saw me and gave me a big hello and a kiss and asked me if my uncle Mike had brought me from Brooklyn. Evidently he had picked up my grandmother from our house in Brooklyn earlier that day, and she was staying with them. I told her no, and then she asked how I got there. I said I walked. She looked at me for a second and then smacked me across the face and told me not to lie. All the relatives were

Uncle Mike and little Michael, who just got married

allowed to discipline you. It took one more slap to convince her that I did walk. She took me inside, made me some scrambled eggs, and called my mother. They were the most delicious eggs I had ever eaten. My mother was hysterical, in tears, thinking I had been kidnapped or something. I was surprised to hear that. After all, I had left a note. When I told her where it was, she was so happy to finally get it. Then my father got on the phone, and all he said was, "I'll be right there." Not good. He didn't like to drive anyway, and if he had to go to Long Island to get me, it would be a long ride home. My mother convinced him to let me stay over, so, thankfully, I survived, and my cousins were fun. So that's the

Me and my son a long time ago. I told you we grew up together.

story. I walked from Brooklyn to Long Island when I was ten and I made it.

Whenever my mother would tell this story, she added a part about my brother, Matty. While I was missing, relatives and friends came to the house and people were actually searching the neighborhood for me. My brother, who was about six at the time, was looking for me as well. He would walk up our street, Euclid Avenue, make a right onto Etna Street, another right onto Pine Street, another right onto Ridgewood Avenue, and then one last right back onto Euclid Avenue, all the while looking in garbage cans and sewers and places where we used to hide when we played. Then he would go into the house and report to our mother that he hadn't found me. He did this over and over and kept going in to Mom and saying the same thing. Finally, after hours of this, and by this time she was very emotional, she snapped at him and said, "Matty, you are driving me crazy. Why do you keep looking in the same places?" Little Matty answered, "I'm not allowed to cross the street."

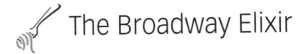

The Broadway Elixir

As my son said earlier in the book I was just on Broadway in *The Producers*. I played Max Bialystock. (Who says I have no range?) It is a very demanding role in every way, and it is very hard on your voice. Doing any part in a Broadway show eight times a week is tough, but Max is one of the toughest. At the beginning of the run, I was having some trouble with my voice, especially on the days we had to do it twice. I was complaining about it to the woman who does my nails. My dear Natasha. She is a Russian émigré, a great manicurist and person. She said she had something that would help my throat. The next day she dropped off a bottle of brown liquid. It wasn't the best-looking stuff, but I tasted it and it was better than it looked, and it really worked. I started making it all the time even when I didn't need it. I think it would taste great on the rocks. It's delicious but not something you want to drink all the time.

1 aloe plant
3 tablespoons honey

1 tablespoon butter
5 ounces Cognac

Cut off a small piece of the aloe plant. Slice the piece open and scrape out the inside. This should yield about 2 tablespoons' worth. Put it in a small saucepan. Add the honey, butter, and Cognac. Heat, while stirring, until it is hot enough to melt the aloe without burning off too much of the liquor. Pour into a bottle and sip.

Ooh, it's good.

ACKNOWLEDGMENTS
AND A STORY

We've been thinking about how to close the book. My son suggested that we thank all the people who helped us. We would have to start with the wives, Julie and Tracy. Our kids, Nicholas and Emily. My Hilda and Beatrice. Jennifer Carrillo, who took the pictures. My agent, Mel Berger, who started this whole thing. Our editor and publisher. My son's friend Charles for his tech help. My cousins Vivian and Barbara for some of the family pictures. My brother, Matty, for the pictures he came up with and for all the eating he did. He was a one-man cheering section as well. We thank everyone for their help and support.

Now that we have taken care of that, we decided to close with one more story about Marc's grandfather, my father, Matty. This story also gives a sense of the kind of place we come from.

In Brooklyn you were from a neighborhood, and that neighborhood would be tight-knit. My father was working and

Four fashion plates, and all together

living back in the old neighborhood in an apartment on the corner of Fulton Street and Nichols Avenue. I was in my second year of the show *Taxi*. It was a big hit and, to tell the truth, I was starting to think who I was. People were asking for my autograph and would I take pictures, and it started to go to my head. I was talking to my father on the phone from Los Angeles, and he asked me to come visit him. I said, "Dad, it's tough for me now. People want autographs and it's hard for me to walk down the street." I could picture his face when he said, "Cut the bull and come to Brooklyn."

A few days later I made the trip. I flew into New York at night so I could sneak into the neighborhood. Of course, I took the biggest limo I could find. I got to my dad's place, and it was great to be there with him. The next day my friend Joey

Mook came over. He suggested we paint my father's apartment. To get the paint, he said we could walk right down Fulton Street to the Pittsburgh Paint store. I said, "Joey, you don't understand how hard it will be for me to just walk around like that. People want pictures. It's too hard." He said, "Cut the bull and let's get the paint."

It was a gorgeous spring day, and Fulton Street couldn't have been busier. People were sitting outside, shoppers shopping, kids riding bikes and playing games, women breast-feeding babies, bedlam. We go down the street walking toward the store, which was a couple of blocks away. No one, nobody, recognizes me. I take that back—nobody even notices me. It gets to the point that I am trying to make eye contact with people, so that someone will see me. People are even coming up and saying hello to Joey but not to me. I started to go a little nuts. It was weird.

We finally got to the paint store, found our paint, and got on line at the cashier. In front of us, on line, were these two twelve- or thirteen-year-old boys; they were buying airplane glue, but that's another story. I thought to myself, these, these are my fans—they'll know me. So I tried to make eye contact, and finally got one of the kids to look at me, but he turned away. That was it. What was going on? It was a little like being in the twilight zone. Well, I couldn't take it anymore. I got the kids' attention and said something I thought I would never hear myself say. It's something that makes me have total disdain for the person saying it. I said, "Don't you know who I am?" One kid looked at me (with disdain) and said,

"Yeah, we know who you are, but your father told us not to bother you."

We hoped you liked the book. It was fun for us to write, and we hope the family is pleased.

So, *mangiamo. Ciao.*

INDEX

Page numbers in *italics* refer to photographs.